Don'
a

BOZANA SKOJO

DON'T GET MAD, GET SUCCESSFUL

BURMANBOOKS
.COM

Published by BurmanBooks Inc.
260 Queens Quay West
Suite 1102
Toronto, Ontario
Canada M5J 2N3

Cover design: Diane Kolar
Photographer: Pirate Pictures
Interior design: Tracey Ogus
Editing: Anna Watson

Distribution:
TruMedia Group LLC
575 Prospect Street, Suite 301
Lakewood, NJ 08701

ISBN 978-1-927005-21-7

Printed and bound in The United States of America

Table of Contents

Dedication

This book is dedicated to my son Matteo. Thank-you for giving me the gift of trust, the gift of true love, and also for shining the light inside me again. My Angel from heaven, you chose me to be your mommy and I can now exhale knowing you are on the other side of my love in a perfect circle of trust, both giving and receiving. You make me laugh so much, and you really have so much personality and charm for such a small little boy. Baki calls you genius baby, and I truly believe you will also do great things with your life, with your hands and your creative mind. I will be there encouraging and loving you every step of the way. I love you more than anything, forever my little boy (boobers and booban) you will be. It is an honour and the greatest blessing of my life to be your mother.

Also, to my mother Iva for your consistent encouragement and devotion. For never letting me think twice about whether you'd be there for me, especially through the roughest times of my life and for saying, "If I could take this from you and go through it myself I would." I look up to your values, your strength and beauty. Thank-you for every home cooked meal, for loving and nurturing your family and loving me, and for being the kind of woman I can look up to. You taught me how to keep good company, eat good foods, the importance of prayer, of having a close family. You showed me how to have the courage to overcome adversity and the inner solitude to turn the other cheek and show restraint. For your resourcefulness, hard work, humility and the way you are always striving to make a better life for yourself; thank-you for teaching me the art of life.

To my step-father Miro for your dedication to our family all these years, and your hard working values. Thank-you for always guiding me towards the right paths, (even if I didn't always listen right away), and always teaching we need to make our own decisions, yet always being there when we fell.

To my brothers Peter and Robert, for being two men in my life I can always count on with both laughter and in need. I know we will be celebrating many years of family tradition together. I love you both and cherish all our memories together. The years keep getting better and better and can't wait to share them with our children.

To my dear and true best friends in this life, thank you all for sharing some of the most amazing moments in my life with me. You are all genuine, beautiful and great women, I will always look to you for guidance and laughter many years to come. I love you all and cherish our unique friendships; Margaret, Silvana, Patrizia, Christina, Kim, Jackie, Terry, Dawn, Roberta, Nadine, Kristina, Colleen, Zoe, Angie, Laura, Billie, Deanna, Dao, Jennifer, Nes, Micheline, Jodi, Michelle, Kendra, and Ali. To my beautiful cousins and family Tomislava, Slavica, and Ivanka, my aunt Anda and Tetko, my Dida Mate, my Stric and Strina and all the other relatives I care for dearly and don't get a chance to see as often, I love you too.

To Grandma Sheila and Grandpa George for being the most loving and amazing grandparents that Matteo could ask for. You are both truly beautiful and special people in both our lives. Thank you for always being there for both of us. He enjoys spending time with you both so much, and is becoming a great little man because of your guidance and love you give.

To my wonderful and gifted staff; Silvana, Lily, Maura, Gigi, Sarah, Marta, Suzanne and Julie. I appreciate your hard work and ethics and I'm looking forward to years of continued success together.

To my colleagues, thank you for lending a helping hand when I needed it, and for all being such wonderful and supportive friends in our businesses together. I am grateful.

To my clients, I also thank you all for your support and continued patronage for all these years. I would not be able to run my business if it weren't for all of you, and it is my pleasure to see so many happy faces walking out our door. Some of you have even become close and dear friends in my life today and I appreciate and I am grateful for our friendships.

To Sanjay Burman, for giving me the opportunity and a new road to self exploration in writing this book and sharing my journeys and my outlook on life, and how you too can overcome any adversity in your life and create the world you have always dreamed of.

To Sanela, Anya and John for helping with editing and writing this book, pushing me forward and to making it fully come to fruition.

To both my father and my grandmother in heaven, thank you for always watching over us. We can all still feel your presence around us and still love you both so much as the days go on.

My recent visit to Croatia, I fell in love with the country once again. I am anxious to return to be with your simplicity and natural beauty, and with the connection to my soul. I feel most at peace when I am there.

And finally to Dean, for conceiving with me the perfect son.

A client of mine long ago gave me this poem, Desiderata. I was feeling down about myself and about life, and I suppose it had showed on my face and my demeanor to everyone who came to see me at work. I wear my heart on my sleeve, so it is hard for me to conceal any emotions at times, especially during a time when I was a bit more timid and didn't understand my true potential. He had written it beautifully in calligraphy and now it hangs in our main treatment room for everyone to appreciate. These words strengthen my resolve for a quality life and I hope they do for you.

DESIDERATA

Go placidly amid the noise and haste,
and remember what peace there may be in silence.

As far as possible without surrender,
be on good terms with all persons.
Speak your truth quietly and clearly;
and listen to others,
even the dull and the ignorant;
they too have their story.

Avoid loud and aggressive persons,
they are vexations to the spirit.
If you compare yourself with others,
you may become vain and bitter;
for always there will be greater and lesser persons than yourself.
Enjoy your achievements as well as your plans.

Keep interested in your own career,
however humble;
it is a real possession in the changing fortunes of time.
Exercise caution in your business affairs;
for the world is full of trickery.
But let this not blind you to what virtue there is;
many persons strive for high ideals;
and everywhere life is full of heroism.

•••

Be yourself.
Especially, do not feign affection.
Neither be cynical about love;
for in the face of all aridity and disenchantment
it is as perennial as the grass.

Take kindly the counsel of the years,
gracefully surrendering the things of youth.

Nurture strength of spirit to shield you in sudden misfortune.
But do not distress yourself with dark imaginings.
Many fears are born of fatigue and loneliness.
Beyond a wholesome discipline,
be gentle with yourself.

You are a child of the universe,
no less than the trees and the stars;
you have a right to be here.
And whether or not it is clear to you,
no doubt the universe is unfolding as it should.

Therefore be at peace with God,
whatever you conceive Him to be,
and whatever your labors and aspirations,
in the noisy confusion of life keep peace with your soul.

With all its sham, drudgery, and broken dreams,
it is still a beautiful world.
Be cheerful.
Strive to be happy.

Max Ehrmann, Desiderata, Copyright 1952.

CHAPTER ONE

We must be willing to let go of the life we have planned, so as to accept the life that is waiting for us.
- *Joseph Campbell*

Faith is the substance of things hoped for, The evidence of things not seen.
- *New Testament - Hebrews 11:1*

THE IMPORTANCE OF BEING A GOOD POOR

From the very beginning I have always been a resourceful person. I looked to myself for solutions to problems and difficulties that I encountered along the way, and drew strength from every obstacle I overcame. The more I looked to my own resources for succour, the stronger I felt and the more confident I became. Over time, this helped to fuel my ambition - if I could rely on myself, who could let me down? I would only ever have myself to blame, and every mistake I made would be a lesson learned.

One of my best friends Patrizia called me 'a good poor' once. It took me some time to figure out what she meant by that. 'A good poor'? I was not sure whether I should be offended or not. I had had a reasonably comfortable upbringing and while I would never describe myself as wealthy, nor had I ever considered myself to be particularly poor. "A good poor?" I asked myself again. What did she mean? When I asked her she only laughed and said I would figure it out one day. I am still not entirely sure what she meant, but I think I have an idea.

It does not matter where I am or what situation I find myself in, I never complain about anything; I pick myself up, put on a little lipstick and get on with it. I think that is what she meant about me being a good poor. Resourcefulness. Resilience. Self-reliance.

I was always resilient in the toughest of times, and I always knew that it was not going be bad forever. I never liked to complain because I knew that you have to get through the bad to reach for the good and that the good is so much better if you know that you were strong the whole journey there and that you did it on your own.

It seems to me that people nowadays give up much too easily; they stumble and falter at the first hurdle, giving up before they have given themselves a real chance to get started. It is one of life's oldest lessons - you will get a few knocks along the way; it is how we learn. But the thing that really sets successful people apart is that they take these blows on the chin and keep on going. If I have been knocked down by circumstance or misfortune, I get right back up on my feet and try to find a new way of meeting the challenge. I was never one of those people who stay down when they meet adversity, and neither are you.

How do I know this? Well, you bought this book and you are reading it. That means you want to help yourself and that you are not relying on other people to find the answers for you. Hopefully, this book will inspire you to get out, change something, go after something, or at the very least give you hope that if you are proactive in your life, things will change.

In many ways, this book is an exploration of what it means to be 'a good poor' because I believe that at the heart of all success must lie an unassailable and unshakable belief in oneself and in one's own ability to overcome adversity and to succeed. I think that those of us who were not fortunate enough to be born with silver spoons in our mouths should all try to be 'good poors'. Being a good poor is about more than simply making the best out of a bad situation; it is about making success out of nothing but your own grit and determination. Just because you have limited resources now, does not mean that you will have limited resources in the future. In this respect, my attitude to life is nothing new - the more you put in, the more you get out. This ethos allows you to start with absolutely nothing but your own resourcefulness and your own initiative. You have a brain, passion and ambition, no one can take that away from you. Your vision for a better tomorrow is yours and yours alone, and only you have the power to make this vision a reality.

This is not your average 'self-help' book. I'm hoping to share some of the lessons I have learned throughout my life. Some of these lessons may seem like common sense, but the process of discovering the truths that lie behind them has been far from straightforward or clear-cut. Writing this book has itself been part of the learning process, and there are many lessons left to be learned. I hope that in sharing my experiences with a wider audience, I can help people to avoid making some of the mistakes I made and find a clearer path to self-fulfillment and happiness.

While much of this book is dedicated to very personal observations and experiences, my professional training and background as an aesthetician gives me a particular perspective on life and personal success. But before you accuse me of simply writing a book just to help you keep up appearances, the following chapters are not about looking good, but about feeling good and succeeding in life.

BOZANA

CHAPTER TWO

LEARNING TO LET GO OF THE PAST

When I was 5 years old, my mother always told me that happiness was the key to life. When I went to school, they asked me what I wanted to be when I grew up. I wrote down 'happy'. They told me I didn't understand the assignment, and I told them they didn't understand life.
~ John Lennon

Be yourself; everyone else is already taken.
- Oscar Wilde

Is it cliché to say time heals all? It does though. No matter what, it does. If you let go of burdens, give your shoulders a chance to breathe, things will work out ok and it is ok not to carry heavy baggage.

I lost my father at a very young age. I was 7 years old, just a few weeks shy of turning 8, and just before Christmas and also my birthday. I'm a Christmas baby, and I had my world tragically end at that very moment he passed away. I realize now that every single experience and decision I made thereafter had come from that moment. I held my breath, and didn't want to let it back out.

I remember my father Mate being a good man, a hard-working man who loved us. He was 36 when he passed on. Thirty-six is young, very young, but being a little girl I had no concept of young and old. It took a long time for me to stop carrying that burden, to stop blaming anyone for him not being here, and to let go that my childhood was left at a standstill. Two decades. The ghost of the past will likely haunt you until you realize that it starts to affect your every day, and your future.

I would dwell on all the things I missed out on with him. I always thought about it, maybe in the hopes that it might bring him back somehow, or keep his memory alive - because I didn't want to forget. I felt sorry for myself and was completely lost. It is like you cannot breathe anymore, when a parent, who is part of your lifeline, someone who is supposed to be on the other end of your love is gone. There isn't anything tangible to catch your thoughts, your needs and your love growing up. It is literally cutting off a limb. Perhaps this is why my love for my son goes beyond anything I have imagined. We are both a part of each others' life lines, and I could never imagine leaving him vulnerable to the world without my love and affection.

Being sad was all I knew from a very young age, numb and sad with walls up. When I examined it from a different perspective as I got older and realized how I'd self-created all the outcomes by my own actions or inactions, and I was amazed at how much power we all hold. It is up to you to make a decision on being sad or miserable for how long, and up to you to take control of your happiness and shift your mind in spite of life's curve balls.

I still feel at times I need to fully exhale, however as more time passes I do breathe easier, after every experience and every lesson learned. I don't hold it in as much. 'It' being anything that has held me back, down, numb and not in control. There isn't a day that goes by that I do not think of what happened, or think of him, or try to grasp at the fading memories that seem so far away in the past. At the time I held his death like a candle. I never burned it out and obsessed about it and it consumed my mind for years. Why did this happen to me? Why me? And again - why me? There were a lot of why me's growing up.

That was the hardest thing that ever happened to me. The aftermath of that single event had drastically changed my life. Initially, it was not for the better, as it created in me a need to protect myself against ever feeling the pain of letting go of someone I love that much. It has been a double-edged sword. I found myself in tremendous fear—fear of having what I want and losing it. It has been a very long journey for me. I've struggled to let go of the belief that if I have someone in my life who I love so completely, they will 'leave.' My commitment to not feel that pain ever again has been a huge hurdle for me.

I think if you experience that sort of pain at a very young age, you have no choice but to grow up - really grow up - deal with it, and use that energy to channel good in your life. You never want to feel that ever again. It is about destiny, *your destiny*, creating yours and leaving a legacy others can be proud of, in spite of anything you feel can be holding you down.

I have been through my share of difficulties since then, however I have learned today to deal with tragedies a little differently, and I learn to let go a little more and know that you have to, if you want to keep moving forward for a fulfilling life. I don't look backwards so much anymore. I have made mistakes later in my life as an adult, including tolerating abuse from former boyfriends because I felt like I could handle it, almost felt comfortable in it (the pain). It somehow felt normal to me. I fit in that space, the numbing mind space, until I couldn't pretend anymore. I also know that you have to give yourself enough time in a 'normal' situation to know the difference.

I remember growing up as a little girl just wanting to be happy, as in the John Lennon quote at the beginning of this chapter. Just happy. The magic of life gives us new beginnings and new hopes, new dreams, new outlooks and new loves. We can choose to see things differently than we used to, and that's ok too. You're allowed to change your mind about how you feel about certain things. It still makes what happened real, and doesn't take away what you felt and went through.

And just sometimes it's ok for the candle to blow out; people need to rest in peace.

CHAPTER THREE

We are what we pretend to be, so we must be careful what we pretend to be.
- Kurt Vonnegut

People come up to me all the time and say "you should be a model," or "you look just like a model," or "maybe you should try to be a man who models." And I always have to laugh because I'm so good looking. Of course I'm a model.
- Derek Zoolander

EARNING MY OWN WAY IN LIFE

As a child, I was always described as pretty. When I became a teenager, the compliments kept coming. By the time I was an adult, people often said I was beautiful. Whether they were right or wrong is not for me to say, but the constant commentary on my physical appearance continues to shape how I think about myself and how I engage with the world around me.

In school, all the pretty girls would talk about the rich husbands they would marry when they grew up. They talked about the nice houses they would live in, the shiny cars they would drive, and the number of dresses they would have in their oversized wardrobes. Growing up, this was nothing out of the ordinary, and my friends continued to dream about their Prince Charmings until well into their adult lives. In fact, one or two eventually found happiness in the arms of well paid city executives and businessmen. Yet, for me, I knew this would not be enough. I knew I wanted more from life than a nice car, dresses, and a big house all paid for by a rich husband. Sure, I wanted all of these things, but I wanted to get them for myself. I knew I had more to offer the world than my looks.

Even back then I understood that looking good was not the same as feeling good. I knew that if I simply followed the same path that society seemed to have laid out for me, no amount of makeup or high heels would ever make me feel truly happy. I needed to find fulfillment through other means than simply marrying a financially well-endowed husband. I had common sense, a good brain, and more importantly, I had ambition and I had passion! So much passion that I truly throw myself into everything I do. When I draw or paint my creativity flows through my fingers. I truly engage myself in every aspect of my life.

I listen to my friends, and I try and give the best advice I can give. I am passionate about their successes and happiness. I love my family dearly, and would do anything to make their lives better and enjoy spending time with them daily. I have loved the relationships I have been in and I completely devote myself body and mind. Perhaps this is why I eventually chose the path of aesthetics later on into my adult life - the bonding with people, making long lasting friendships and the camaraderie. It involves listening, learning, and absorbing as much as I can to try and make things clearer for my client, giving them someone to lean on and talk to. I felt great being a sounding board and making them feel better about themselves going home, feeling prettier or more handsome after our detailing.

Feeling good about yourself imparts its own beauty - a beauty that runs, proverbially, more than skin deep. I recognized early on that people can be more beautiful on the outside if they are happy on the inside. This was perhaps one of the earliest lessons I recall and it continues to underpin my current ethos as a practicing aesthetician.

Even today, people still expect me to find a handsome and rich husband and settle down to a life of placid contentment. People assume that because I am reasonably attractive, I must have less than average intelligence. I am struck by this seemingly ingrained prejudice that I encounter everyday, whether in the workplace, in the media or even in my personal life.

Looking back over the years, it is much easier to impart a sense of meaning, direction and purpose to the events that transpired, but at the time, things always seemed much more haphazard. It is only with hindsight that I recognize the power that this prejudice must have had on me. There is a popular and misguided logic that says you cannot be clever and beautiful. It is almost as if people anticipate some kind of divine or cosmic system of justice - you can only be one or the other, not both - that would be unfair.

Perhaps, in hindsight, I should be thankful for this misconception, for it has undoubtedly spurred me on over the years. I have tried to fight this prejudice in everything I throw myself into, and my personal and professional successes over the years have vindicated my efforts. I wanted people to see me for my brains rather than just my beauty. While I have by no means let this struggle completely define who I am or what I do, I can see that it will always play an important role in shaping my outlook on life, and even to an extent, my very character.

I felt that being successful would actually be my way of sticking up for myself. Hard work and determination would be a catalyst for me in finding myself. I was a shy little girl wanting to hide until I kicked ass in something I knew, something that would transform me and my identity and how people remembered me when they heard my name. So from an early age I looked to the future, looked at what a legacy could mean, looked at how to transform myself and become proficient and win the world with respect. I believe you have to pave your way from the beginning, wherever you choose that to be, and make it true. See it to the end, and know yourself.

You are the only one who knows the truth. I chose not to use my looks to get me through any easy path. I wanted to *feel* confident in a room, because I had earned it.

CHAPTER FOUR

Idle hands, are the devil's workshop.
- Unknown

There are women who, however you may search them, prove to have no content but are purely masks. The man who associates with such almost spectral, necessarily unsatisfied beings is to be commiserated with, yet it is precisely they who are able to arouse the desire of the man most strongly: he seeks for her soul—and goes on seeking.
- Nietzsche

FINDING MY PASSION

I am not sure when I realized what I wanted to be growing up, but I always found a way to get into my mother's makeup bag, even at three years old. I would draw all over myself (and the wall) as children tend to do when they are young. My mother was (and still is) a very beautiful woman and I admire her beauty both inside and out.

She has always taken good care of herself, always left the house with a little makeup, hair nice and never wore drab clothes. Ever. She was always well dressed, which seems natural for me now.

When I was a young woman though, it used to bother me when other people noticed her. They would always say to me, "Your mom's so good looking". I wanted to ignore it and look up to her as a mommy and not simply as an object for the world to stare at.

My mother had always been a hard worker and got up quite early every morning. I helped raise my brother Peter since I was thirteen when he was born. My mother had remarried when I was about 13, and I would take him to daycare early in the mornings before I went to school. My rebellious older brother Robert had moved out when he was in his late teens and my mother had finally got a good job at the hospital, and the only shift that was available was her starting at about 5:30 in the morning. I made sure Peter was up and on his way. This gave my mother the chance to come home early enough to make dinner and pick him up. I saw how hard life was sometimes, the challenges of juggling everything - and I learned that family is always the most important. It gave me responsibility and the fortitude to help my family and I always felt like a second mother to my brother.

I did not come from a lazy family, and I remember the stories my mother used to tell us about my grandmother tilling the farm back in Croatia, and of her walking to school in five feet of snow. I suppose most European families can attest to this and probably have a similar collection of 'when I was your age' stories. Having to work, helping to put food on the table and earning a living for yourself the honest way became a part of contributing to society. If I wanted to buy that new sweater, it was easier to get if I had earned the money myself. It was natural, and I have had jobs of one sort or another since I was 15. I've never had a break from work since then.

I worked cash at the supermarket, served meals to patients at the hospital, worked at different retail stores selling clothes, and have also been a waitress and bartender. One way or another, I was always serving the community. Working with people in a hands-on fashion was easy. With the bartending came listening to my guests which I enjoyed as well. I felt that people needed to get away from the humdrum of everyday life, and sometimes they needed to get things off their chests to a complete stranger.

I was actually bartending when I discovered that there was a school that had just opened nearby which offered a program called 'aesthetics and cosmetology'. What is this I wondered? I spent five years after I graduated high school not knowing what I really wanted to do, and not finding my vocation, my calling. When I heard of this program for the first time, I knew it was for me even though I had no real idea what it was about but it called to me. Starting from that first semester I knew that I would fire my way through the course kicking its ass and I knew I would get the top grade. I don't know how, but I just did. When there's something that you love or feel connected to, you need to put your whole heart into it. I found my passion, and I asked question upon question until I knew everything about the aesthetics and beauty industry. I finally knew what I was meant to do, as the program did call to me, and I put my heart and soul into everything I adore.

I finished with a 98% average, and to be honest the missing 2% bugged me. I was on the Dean's List, finished with Honours and won Student Of The Year after my graduation ceremony out of almost 100 students enrolled. It was my time to feel good about things. I felt that I had waited for so long for something like this, and I was so proud to have earned it. When the Dean of the school had given me my award he held up a video I had done when I was on CityLine television, a local talk show. I had still been in school and a reputable hairdresser who was a regular on the show for Fashion Fridays had so loved the makeup I had done for an interview that he asked me to be on the show. I was thrilled. Everyone at the restaurant I was working at watched me on TV. I could taste success.

Since I had always been in the service industry and people were always either telling me their life stories or needing advice, being an aesthetician came naturally. But listening to people is only one part of being a good aesthetician. I believe you have to try and look the part, and be the part. Just as you would like to go to a hairdresser with nice hair, if you are an aesthetician, keeping your skin clean, wearing a little makeup and looking polished and confident brings that out in others. I love wearing makeup, love getting dressed up and helping other women to look and feel their best. It made me feel great having someone look towards me, and ask how I had done something with my makeup, my skin, my glow. I liked this kind of attention as I was combining beauty with knowledge.

I had just broken up with my boyfriend after my graduation from aesthetics school, and I found a place to move into by myself to clear my head of the long-term dead-end relationship. It was the basement of my mother's good friend's house. She was a super lady and I was very comfortable to be there. It was scary at first to be out in the world by myself, but that was what needed to happen.

LEARN ALL YOU CAN

One of the most important chapters in my life is the time I spent working at Salon Marc. It was there that I really began to learn my trade and develop meaningful relationships with clientele. I suppose you could say that it taught me all the basics of the beauty industry. It was like being at college in that respect, but it was so much more than that too. During the years I worked at Salon Marc I met some incredible people who, over time, I came to see as my family.

While I worked at Marc's I was happy to be embarking on an important step in life. I was earning money, gaining experience, and more importantly winning the respect of my clients and those who worked in the industry. At first it felt so good to be making a living by doing something I enjoyed so much. I was making people look and feel beautiful, and let me tell you, seeing the smiles on the faces of all my clients after their treatment was like a drug to me. I knew I was good at my job, but to see so many people come back and ask for me to treat them again was just great. I was slowly finding my niche.

I started working in the basement of the salon shortly after graduation from aesthetics school. It was my first real job in the beauty industry and I was itching to get started. My course had taught me a great deal of theory and even though we had a lot of hands-on workshops, I could hardly wait to get started on a real client.

At first, I remember filing nails in the basement of the salon, and sitting around waiting for clients. The business was fairly small to begin with and I had a lot of time to think about how I would like to start my own business one day. Of course, at this stage I did not really have a clear idea about how I could actually start my own spa, but I knew if I kept my eyes open I would find the answers. I decided then and there that I would use my time at Salon Marc to learn about every aspect of the business from filing nails to filing financial reports. It would be my postgrad degree.

I used the quiet time between clients thinking about how I wanted to build up my clientele and I spent many hours dreaming about how busy it would be for me one day. Even though some of the small jobs were less glamorous than I would have liked, I knew that if I ever wanted to run my own business, I would have to be an expert in every single aspect of my work. More importantly, I realized that being at the bottom of the pile would make me a better manager of people in the long run. I would be able to understand their concerns and expectations and if need be, put a comforting hand on their shoulder and say, "I've been there too". I never want to lose sight of my first few months at Salon Marc. Humility is everything. I remember thinking that if I ever started a business I would make sure that I gave each and every one of my employees the kind of training that would help them to realize their own goals. I would never become detached from any part of my business.

I remember that the manager who hired me raved about how the owner of the salon was going to turn the upstairs level (where he lived) into a spa one day. I admired his vision and business acumen. Here was a man worth looking up to. At last, here was a good role model for me. What could he teach me? How can I learn from him? For the first few years I kept my head down and worked hard to bring in new business and ensure that our clients kept coming back. I could see that Marc's plan to expand into the floor above us depended entirely on our ability to make money and retain customers. I was a small fish in a big pond, but I knew that every dollar I made was bringing Marc closer to his dream.

As it turned out, it took about three or so years for us to be able to expand the business. During that time, I continued to earn the trust and respect of our growing client base, and more and more people started coming through our doors. It was so rewarding to see our hard work pay off. We invested care, skill and expertise into every job, no matter how trivial, and our clients recognized our passion for the work.

Marc was excited to expand the business, but since he was a hairdresser by profession he did not know very much about aesthetics. So, he took me further into his confidence and left that side of the business to me. I ordered everything from the furnishings to the technical equipment and supplies. I must have been as excited as Marc. I had almost four years worth of experience and I felt like I was moving on and moving up in the world. The only thing that was not moving up at this time was my monthly paycheque. I had serviced clients impeccably for four years and everyone raved about my services. People started to recognize my name on the circuit and customers would keep coming back to the spa and ask for me personally. Heck, I had even been dubbed the 'eyebrow queen'.

Finally, in my fourth year I decided to write a letter to Marc, expressing my concern and laying out on paper why I deserved a raise after all that time. I had a great deal of respect for Marc and I certainly did not want to be confrontational, but you have to stick up for yourself. You cannot rely on other people to fight your corner.

My reasoning was fairly straightforward and I thought I made a compelling argument. I had continually taken classes at my own expense from Aveda. It was a necessity; as an Aveda Concept Salon we needed to have the same service custom as all spas under their wing. The cost of a single class was typically around $100-500, so I spent thousands on my own training post graduation. Even though I had taken the classes on my own initiative, I argued that the courses directly benefitted Salon Marc because the more qualified I became, the more services we could offer to our customers. I wanted to make a name for myself in the beauty industry, so I threw myself at all the events and shows I could find. Publicity for me also meant publicity for Salon Marc. I wrote that I was an invaluable asset to the company and that I should be paid accordingly.

I was always one of the top sellers in retail every month and I helped to build the entire spa, even getting involved with designing the layout of the new workspace so that we could utilize the area most effectively. In addition, I reminded Marc that I had I created all of the service and product menus every year, editing them word for word. Since we offered so many services, this was a very time consuming process, especially since it had to be perfect.

I had been asked to be the face of the salon in endorsements on television on the local news channel and morning shows. No one else had felt comfortable or interested and Marc had asked me to represent the workplace and be the spokesperson, talking about the beauty industry. I felt very comfortable doing this, at first with a few little butterflies in my stomach but it was where I felt natural and ought to be. I didn't mind being in front of the camera, as it gets easy enough speaking about things you already know. It's the wider live audience staring at you that can debilitate people sometimes.

As if these were not reasons enough for a pay rise, I also reminded Marc that I had designed the website from scratch and managed online content, all in my own time in the evenings after work. I wanted everything to be perfect, just as if I was running my own business. I felt personally invested in Salon Marc, and proud that we were becoming an increasingly successful business. I told Marc all of these things, and I told him I had never once been compensated for the time, money and effort I had put into the company. I do not doubt for second that Marc recognized and valued my input - I know how much he appreciated it. Even the smallest things take so much time and effort to get right.

My letter had the desired effect, and I was then given a three dollar raise, one dollar for every year I had worked at the spa. I was now on $14 per hour plus a small commission only if I exceeded my paycheque in revenue service. I loved the idea of working for commission because I knew I was good at my job.

I was naturally talented at bringing out the beauty in others. I loved seeing how the subtle hints and tones of makeup could bring out the beauty in a face. I loved to see how a brush stroke here or a pencil line there could accentuate the natural harmony between features. I was an artist. I still am.

I had always been artistic since I was a child and it has been a gift I have had all my life. Some people have a natural flair for music, some for athletics. From as early as I can even remember, I always adored art and was completely lost in my artwork whenever I had the chance. It had always been my favourite subject even as a small child well into high school. I had always been able to replicate an image before me, and loved over the years being able to use the gift to turn my hands and energy into art.

My natural understanding of colours, form and the aesthetic ideal meant that being a makeup artist came naturally to me. Once I have a brush in my hand, I just let my instinct take over. I paint by feeling and intuition. I study the face for a moment, try to understand the person underneath and then my brush takes over. I do not need to think rationally or logically. I do not need theory to guide me now.

I like to think that Picasso and Monet would

have been equally good makeup artists - only our canvasses are different.

MAKING AND KEEPING FRIENDS

I consider the people I worked with at Salon Marc as my family. After seven years of working in a close team of highly gifted beauty artists I came to know and care for each and every one of them. Seeing the same 15 plus faces for almost 2,500 days is pretty intense and you obviously forge lasting relationships and close bonds.

Over time, I came to love them and know them like they were members of my own family. Sure, we argued and fought from time to time, but I challenge you to find me siblings that do not. We laughed and cried together, experienced life in its myriad shades and drew strength from each other in times of strife and difficulty. Together we went through the ups and downs of relationships, work stress, family stress, happy occasions, weddings, births, deaths, parties, staff parties, summer get-togethers everything that friends do together and everything you would invite a loved one to.

The close working relationship we had at Salon Marc meant everything to me. It showed me that work does not have to be a place of arduous toil and drudgery. If you follow your dreams and dare to walk your own path you will quickly find that you will always be surrounded by like-minded people. Maybe that is why we all got on so well together. We were artists, each in our given field of expertise, and we thrived in an atmosphere of creativity and flair.

Do not be put off if you find yourself in a new job feeling uncertain and nervous. It takes time to build up a meaningful rapport with your colleagues - this is why it is so important to follow your vision and work in an area that you are passionate about. I love working in the beauty industry, so I have lots of common ground with those I work with. Find your niche and embrace it. Be positive and kind and people will gravitate towards you.

TEAMWORK

Do you ever wonder why cafes and bars that are so close to each other all stay in business? People think you need to open up shop somewhere far away from your competition. Why? Why not open up on the same street? That isn't so bad. We had 14 spas or salons within a 3 block radius of Salon Marc, and I don't remember one business ever closing down. Do you know what it did? It brought *awareness* to that core, and it became the street where you could get your hair, nails, massage, laser or whatever done. I remember even referring clients down the street for an appointment if they needed one right away and we were all booked up. People will come back to you because they like you. And one salon cannot cut the entire city's hair. It's ridiculous.

We need competition, and a little competition is good for everyone. It is the camaraderie that I talked about that sets you apart from the rest. Be bigger than that and you should never show fear of losing your business or clients, because if you are already in that mindset then I'm sure your clients are already looking elsewhere. Fourteen salons on practically the same street makes everyone busy, just as fourteen cafes on the same street makes all the cafes busy. If one is booked up, then try the next. Same goes for our motto at the spa we worked at. Why does it matter who is sitting in your chair? *Someone* is sitting there. As long as every stylist and every aesthetician has a client sitting in his or her chair is what matters.

We trained clients to feel that way too. They never felt intimidated about trying someone else. Sometimes you want to, and don't want to offend the person that did your hair or nails last. This system eliminated all of that, so that it was just about getting the person in as quickly as possible and what time they wanted best. If there was a request for a specific technician, then obviously they were booked. I loved working like that, and we all worked so well together and had always complemented our work together and timed our consecutive client appointments so well. We all knew who took long talking to their client, who was faster at certain services, who could whip up a quick makeup application and so on - we all knew all our strengths and weaknesses and we never tried to show any confusion to any client. We always made something work, even if they showed up thinking they had an appointment on a day they didn't, we made it happen. I counted one time over 100 years of teamwork. That was how long we collectively had all worked together, and it was one of the only salons that had never had a high turnover as most do.

ALWAYS MAKE AS BIG AN ENTRANCE AS POSSIBLE

Starting out in the beauty industry I wanted to make the most of every opportunity and earn some recognition from the wider beauty community. I thought that the best way of doing this would be through direct competition with other artists. I could prove to myself how good I was and show the world that I meant business.

I entered my first competition in *Canadian Hairdresser Magazine* for Makeup Artist Of The Year. We hired a professional photographer I had researched who often submitted photographs to these kinds of contests. We took three before-and-after shots and sent these straight to the magazine. In due course, and to my elation, I was notified that I had become a top 10 finalist in the competition, and I was invited to the gala award show where they would announce the winner. I was beside myself with excitement. I was shortlisted in my first competition, and a prestigious one at that too!

The award show recognizes all types of hairdressing, including colouring and various style categories, but only one makeup category. The whole event was an eye-opener. I saw so many talented artists and made some great contacts for the future. In the end, after all the excitement, I did not win first place. I was obviously a bit disappointed but I was proud of myself for making it this far on my first attempt.

It was incredible to feel a part of an industry that is so passionate about creating beauty and about celebrating our skills and getting together. I felt truly privileged to be there. I know a lot of people say that it is not all about winning and taking first place, but I really did feel like a winner because I had been shortlisted. I did not re-enter the competition again because other projects I was involved with took precedence, but this is certainly something I will come back to. The judges had seen what I was capable of, they obviously liked my work and they could see my potential.

I remember reading about the hairdressers and makeup artists who were really making it big in magazines. Some treated celebrities and were at the forefront of the industry. I had noticed and looked up to one in particular, Jie and thought to myself that I would be working by his side one day. He was crowned the King of Hairdressers and had been doing various celebrities, actresses and models - even Ivana Trump. Little did I know our paths would indeed cross one day years later and I would have the privilege of working beside an energetic and passionate artist for over a year who commanded $400 per haircut. I even got to have Nelly Furtado as a client because of our mutual workspace. It is true that you can dream, and dream BIG!

BOZANA

CHAPTER FIVE

A little less conversation, a little more action.
– Elvis

Entrepreneurship is living a few years of your life like most people won't, so that you can spend the rest of your life like most people can't.
- Unknown

BUILDING FOR THE FUTURE

I had always wanted to own my own spa from the beginning, to make my clients feel comfortable in the hands of any one of my staff members, as they would all be handpicked by me and trained by me. I think if you run a tight ship and do not hold people hostage to your business, they will actually stay and not plot to make their escape. I think if you give to your employees and make an environment pleasing to stay, they stay. You should want your staff to want to be there. I think bosses forget that they were employees once, dreaming about opening a business for themselves.

There are also employees that are workers and just love to punch the clock in/out and live life that simply.

They know what time they finish and start what they will make for the rest of their lives and that's ok too. We all have a different dream and we all want the quality of our life to improve. There are those who also take action towards pursuing their dreams and that's what makes the biggest difference in moving forward. Yes - action, physically going out there and paving the way to your own success. Everyone gets scared at times, but when it comes to a plan, having a vision and making it work, implementing your talents and going for it, then you shouldn't be scared. This is the moment you have always dreamed of and it's exciting! Just do it. It doesn't matter if you might fail along the way or have a setback. People fail and still keep moving, keep dreaming and keep trying. You need to believe in yourself before anyone else is going to believe in you.

This was the very foundation of me wanting my own business - my own laser hair removal equipment to be exact. I had worked at Salon Marc for a few years and needed to challenge my mind and my talents. I was getting a little bored and feeling too much like I was settling into a routine, and I needed and craved the opportunity to learn something new. The office manager of a local dermatologist was a client of the salon, and she mentioned that they were looking for a new laser technician. It was exactly what I was looking for at that point and I was excited to set foot into a renowned dermatologist's office and learn the new and growing field of medical aesthetics. I worked there part-time for almost two years, operating a laser hair removal machine called the LightSheer Diode laser, treating patients and even traveling to various other doctors' offices that had contracted the use of her laser. I was working six days a week, alternating between Salon Marc and Dr. Zara's. I stayed in my field but the beauty of the beauty industry is that it is so vast. You can take that diploma and do so many things with it. You have to create your career and vocation. I was doing just that.

PRACTICE WHAT YOU PREACH

By now, you are probably aware of the value I place on self-reliance. But, as with everything, it is always far easier to write about these attributes than to actually use them in day-to-day life. Being self-reliant requires a conscious effort. You cannot simply be self-reliant at first. Over time, and with dedication, this will become your default setting. At first you will have to make choices that may sometimes seem to be better in principle than reality. Becoming self-reliant is a long-term investment in your life skills. This means that you may have to make short-term sacrifices for long-term gains. So while you should always be looking for opportunities, avoid simply being opportunistic. Be prepared to play the long game.

Even though I always had the aim of starting up on my own, I never solicited any business from any of the dermatologist's patients, even though I knew many of them would be the very clients I would later hope to win once I started up on my own. Remember what I said earlier about creating networks of friends and opportunities - well, I never wanted the doctor, someday down the road, to think that I had been sneaking in the treatment room telling patients that I was buying a laser and that they should come see me in the future.

The truth is, a lot of people in the industry do just that, and wouldn't have a problem with soliciting clients from a current employer. It is part of the whole 'my client/my patient' attitude. In my view, the patients/clients belong to the business or practice and not the specific person who treats them. Until you go through the blood, sweat and tears of opening your own business, you do not have the right to call them your own clients, or clients rather to take away from the establishment. Of course we develop relationships with the people we service over the years (in fact, this is an essential part of a successful business - you have to actively work hard to build these relationships) and some clients do come back to see a certain technician personally, but I firmly believe that you should never cross the line of trust with an employer by biting the hand that feeds you.

This goes for all areas of life. Listen to your parents; through their support and advice, they feed you. Listen to your boss; through paycheques and career development, they too feed you too. And if you don't like where you work, then there are always other possibilities out there, you just need to find your niche.

In this case, I just could not bite the hand that was feeding me. My employer had worked hard to win the patient base we enjoyed, and I saw them as her reward and not mine. I knew that when I started my own business that I would feel proud of each and every one of my clients as each one would be testimony to my success. I am a strong believer that what goes around, comes around, and I did not want to build my future off the back of someone else's success or through what I considered to be bad practice.

Instead, trusting in myself as always, I preferred leaving my job altogether to start out afresh on my own, keeping my good name and my integrity. I try to be honourable in everything I do.

By leaving my job in this way I was maintained a good professional relationship with my employer and avoided burning any bridges. I knew that my course of action would be respected, and by not poaching existing clients from my old job, that I had forged a lasting bond in the industry. My employer knew that the only reason I left was because of my desire to work for myself, something I have been passionate about since the day I graduated from school.

In fact, even at school, I knew that I wanted to work for myself as soon as possible - it is all part of being self-reliant I guess. In class, my peers must have picked up on my self-confidence and self-reliance, and would often look up to me for guidance and support with their work. My aesthetics instructor Zoe said when I graduated, that I would one day surpass all my instructors in success. I was naturally flattered by the compliment but I knew that I would have to work hard in order to become successful. Nothing comes for free.

When I quit performing laser treatments at Dr. Zara's, I knew I could do it alone, and I was ready to take the final leap and put my money where my mouth was. I did not want to talk about it any more. Following through on my decision to start my own business was one of my first gambles, and I never looked back.

STARTING OUT BY MYSELF

My decision to start my own business was also driven by some fairly rational number crunching.

I was working very hard and not really reaping much of the revenue. When I calculated what revenue the facility brought in just from laser hair removal patients, it was ten times what I was I made for working there two days a week. I was doing all of the treatments, re-booking the clients, doing all the consultations, upselling to larger treatment packages, traveling with the laser to several other doctors' offices in several cities, not to mention being pleasant and friendly to all patients, working hard, not complaining and being as efficient as I could.

One day it occurred to me that if I was essentially running all aspects of the business, what was to stop me doing all of this for myself and reaping the benefits of my hard work directly? I already had almost two years' experience of managing critical business operations in the industry and was thoroughly trained in laser treatments. I had all the skills I needed. After some careful reflection I realized that the only thing I did not physically have was a laser machine.

In my job I had been fortunate and lucky enough to have worked with a machine that was superior to all other lasers on the market; it was the gold standard in laser hair removal, and was built from the ground up specifically for that service. I had worked with the LightSheer Diode laser machine for two years and had seen first hand the beautiful results I was able to achieve on hundreds of patients. As far as I could see, it was a no-brainer which laser I should buy.

BUYING A LASER

You might ask yourself what possible reason I have for telling you how to go about buying a laser hair removal machine. Please bear with me. I am fairly sure that you are not looking to buy a laser hair removal machine, but this small episode taught me a lot about self-reliance and perseverance. Every step of the way, there was a new challenge, and every step of the way demanded a new solution.

Each state in the U.S has its own regulations so I needed to be thorough in researching which rules applied to my situation prior to starting the business. No one had the answers I was looking for, so I spent many a frustrating hour on the internet learning all that I could about owning and operating medical laser equipment. In the end, I found that if you have the money and wish to own a laser removal machine here in Canada, you simply buy it through the distributor. It is as simple as that!

The only disadvantage is that you only get half day to a full day's worth of training on the equipment, from the distributor, which is obviously insufficient time to be trained on any medical equipment. It made me appreciate the knowledge and experience I had already had under my belt! In addition, I was only given the theoretical grounding in operating the machine rather than the kind of hands-on training I expected.

There has been talk for years about this becoming a more regulated industry, however as this is a non-surgical treatment then a 'medical aesthetician' or other provider can essentially perform these treatments. In the long term, the country may require the involvement of a Medical Director, however this hasn't transpired in the now 17 plus years since I first started my career.

SECURING RESOURCES

Once I realized the potential, my next challenge was to find the money to pay for the laser. Once again, I resorted to some good old-fashioned number crunching. The original cost I was quoted for the laser itself was $70,000 US, but after looking at the various options more closely, I realized that the cost of actually owning and operating a laser would be much more than this. There were buyout options to consider, exchange rates to factor in, warranty payments and other lease arrangements to consider, plus interest charges. The total cost for a LightSheer laser came to something close to $202,000CAD, almost twice as much as I had expected! My family and friends strongly advised against the leasing option and suggested instead that I try a little smaller venture. I decided to ignore their advice. Yes, I was crazy, but I really wanted to do this alone.

Once I had figured out the cost, I sat down again with a pen, paper, and much used calculator in order to work out how to make my money back once I had signed on to a lease agreement.

This kind of exercise can be extremely daunting, especially if you do not have a background in accounting or math, but with a little application and self-belief, not to mentioned several cups of coffee, all you have to do is break it down into smaller, bite-size goals. If you chip away at big challenges one small part at a time, you will quickly find that you have resolved the whole problem.

Looking at the huge figure of $202,000 on the paper in front of me, I was not sure where to begin. How on earth was I going to make that kind of money?

I returned to first principles. I make money from my clients. How much does a single course of laser treatment cost? How many clients do I need to make up the money? Looking at it like this made it much easier to understand in real terms.

I worked out how many 'bikini clients' I needed to pay it off, and on this basis, I figured I needed 202 women at $1,000 each to pay off the machine. When I looked at the picture in that aspect instead of, 'oh my God I have to pay a small condo off in 3 years', it made sense. I was never really scared. I knew I could do it.

When I looked at all the successful business owners around me I wondered what they had that I did not and realized that the answer was nothing. Their success came from their own self-motivation and drive. I was self-motivated and driven so I could do it too. I found that all these successful business people had simply implemented their thoughts and turned them into actions. They had already taken the first steps that I was about to make.

When I finally signed the agreement I was very happy to have made a decision and followed through with it.

MANAGING PRESSURE

In the beginning working for myself was hectic. Not

quite chaotic, but pretty close let me tell you. My bills at the very beginning exceeded $10,000 per month. That was what I had to make to break even and pay all my bills and expenses for the month. My lease rate just for the laser alone exceeded $3,500 per month. I had received a personal loan for $35,000 from the bank as a down payment for the machine and to help with startup costs. I couldn't get more than that. I was also able to get 2 lines of credit a short time later, and a couple of credit cards, yet I made sure that I never missed a single payment. Independence is everything to me.

With all this money coming in and going out it was vital to keep a close eye on everything in case I made a mistake. Again, I treated this huge task as a series of small bite-size operations. I prioritized my expenses according to the dates they were due and I quickly learned how to balance the books in a small private enterprise. Administration is a crucial part of any business, and while I am not particularly fond of spending hours a day tapping away at a spreadsheet, I was just excited to be exerting myself in the pursuit of my own goals. I was finally happy to use my resources and my patience and love for my career to do something rewarding that would benefit me in the end. It was easy enough to work out of Salon Marc when I began my venture. I had arranged a commission on laser treatments with Marc instead of having the extra expense of leasing a room in another spa or storefront. I had to try and keep my overhead as low as possible and the one piece of equipment was literally draining me at times. I couldn't afford anything else in my life those first couple of years.

I had even moved back into my parents' house for two years as I couldn't afford to live on my own anymore. I decided to forego my personal space for a more rewarding near future. I remember never even walking into a mall for over two years, as I obviously could not afford to buy anything, ever. Each dollar I earned I had to pay off in one bill that seemed to creep up on me every other day.

It is so important in life to recognize your strengths and weaknesses, but you should never let them determine the course of your life. Your goals should drive you. My goal was to start my own beauty practice, and I was not going to let piles of bills and tedious administration stand in the way of success.

Securing and purchasing this one piece of equipment would be the bread and butter of my future goal of opening a larger facility and hiring staff. I wanted to pay off the laser and start my own practice down the road. I had already incorporated my new company, Laser Spa Group with the intention of franchise the business and take it to great levels one day. I researched business licenses on the internet, including the difference between sole proprietorship and incorporations, and went to a lawyer in town to finalize the paperwork and incorporate my brand.

Starting out alone was the biggest step of my life. There was nothing to stop me but my own self-doubt and insecurity. Once you make the first step you too will see that there is no going back. You do not have to start your own business to realize that taking responsibility for your own life and acting on your decisions will lead to happiness and fulfillment. You have the power within you to decide what is right for you. The lessons I learned from starting up my business continue to shape my outlook on life. Never give in; trust your instincts; never lose sight of your goals; make changes one step at a time and if you come up against a brick wall, chip away at it piece by piece rather than throwing yourself against it with all your strength.

SELF-RELIANCE

Finding a healthy role model is one thing, but relying on them is quite another. In fact, I don't like to rely on anyone, whether they are my role model or not, unless I really have to. For example, if I ever needed a loan or help with starting my business, the Laser Spa Group, I did not want to put the burden on anyone else. This was my endeavour, my initiative and my business. I wanted to be in absolute control from start to finish.

One particular example comes to mind. When I bought my laser, rather than borrow money from a bank, friend or family member, I decided that it would be better to pay rent on hired equipment than be indebted to a third party.

From the very beginning, friends and family counseled against this course of action. They thought it would be better to seek financial support in order to buy my own laser and pay back the interest over time. I didn't really have anyone saying they would lend me $200k either; it's hard sometimes the route one must follow. But right from the start, I knew that I did not want to rely on anyone else. Self-reliance had got me to the point of feeling ready to take on the challenges of starting a new business, so there was no reason to think that self-reliance would not hold the key to success further down the line. At this point, I was the only person who could see the long-term vision of my business.

Never be pig-headed or stubborn, and always be prepared to listen to the advice of your friends, but if you really believe that you know better, go with it. You are the best judge of yourself. You know you.

Despite my belief in my own vision and my own ability to make this a reality, I still craved some kind of endorsement from my contemporaries. Instead, anyone I spoke to said I was crazy. All I had needed was for one person to say it was okay, or that it was a good idea. Even though I was confident of my decision, it makes a huge difference to have someone else agree with you. At the time, the only person who had offered me the kind of verification I wanted was my dentist. I had visited my dentist for some years so he knew me fairly well.

Dr. Amato was well liked and admired by everyone I spoke to and that knew him. His practice reminded me of Salon Marc where I was currently working; you could feel the energy and the vibe from his office and you could tell that everyone that worked there actually liked being there. Everyone knew you when you came in and I always felt really great and really important, like I mattered when I left. He was handsome, charming, smart, polite and everything you would want to look up to in a boss, (or so it seemed from my perspective). Ok so maybe I had a crush on him too, but I think every girl did.

When those words came from Davide Amato - that

he thought I should do it and work for myself - it meant everything. It was just what I needed to know that I was not crazy. It meant so much to me that this person saw a glimpse of my desire and my aspirations and thought I should do it. Anything anyone else said after that didn't matter.

He had grappled with the trials and tribulations of starting an independent business; he had experienced the sleepless nights worrying about finances; he had invested his own money and put his livelihood on the line all for a vision that he, and no one else, had. His words strengthened my resolve.

The experience taught me that when you ask for advice, you have to understand the context in which it is given, and rate the value of that advice accordingly. In this case, my family and friends were understandably concerned that I would waste my money on leasing fees without investing in a permanent business asset as in a small aesthetic room with small clientele. I had already negotiated a buyout option after the lease expiry, which meant I would then finally own my equipment. This would be the start of my first business asset. They were worried that I would get hurt somewhere along the line and worried that I would be exposing myself to unnecessary risk. People who care about you - particularly friends and family - are more likely to dwell on the possible risks of a certain course of action than the possible rewards. This is entirely natural, but sometimes you have to take risks that other people might find unacceptable. As I said before, you know you better than anyone else, and only you have the vision for your future.

If you want to get more objective advice, seek out those who have experienced first hand the kind of situation in which you are likely to find yourself. In other words, seek out the experts. In my case, it was my dentist who had started up a business alone.

Nevertheless, whether I had received the endorsement of my dentist or not, my mind was already made up. No one was going to change my mind. Ultimately, the only thing you should rely on is your own intelligence or resourcefulness – not your family, your looks, your boyfriends, husbands or friends.

After experiencing several setbacks in my life, and in the chapters to come, I look back now at the previous excerpt about Dr Amato and how he had also put his livelihood on the line for a different career and a new vision years later. When you are a hardworking entrepreneur, you don't just 'stop'. People think that when you own your own business you will hire others to do the work and you will reap the benefits. It boggles my mind. Your work evolves and you never really stop funneling your energy into your business, as you shouldn't ever stop investing into yourself either. It never stops.

So when I heard years later that Dr Amato had sold his practice and invested his entire life savings of $17 million as well as his family's and friends' investments to a scam invester and financial advisor, I was a little stunned at first at his actions and that a big piece of the pie (the most important piece) wouldn't be there at the office where I enjoyed going so much. The fraudulent investor that eventually conned them all, including Davide, into a sort of 'ponzi scheme' ended up killing himself and leaving Davide and many others baffled at the events that transpired. I remember feeling sick to my stomach that something like this could happen, and always it seems to happen to good people. When life seems to hit hard, and it will at some point in someone's life and something bad happens you have three choices. You can either let it define you, let it destroy you, or you can let it strengthen you.

I remember having a dream and wanting to speak to Davide after that had happened. I couldn't help but just say something to him even if it was just 'it's going to be ok', because I had appreciated his friendship, looked up to him as a good man and his advice when I had needed it. I wasn't even sure if my advice had even mattered at all, or my concern. But I had to know that suicide wasn't an option for him, as that was something people had been talking about. He said that thought had never even crossed his mind, and that he still had his two bare hands to work with and his mind, which was what had created his wealth in the first place. He would continue practicing dentistry and day by day get through the terrible black hole that he and so many others had found themselves in. I admire him now even more.

<u>CHAPTER SIX</u>

Nothing splendid has ever been achieved
Except by those who dared believe
That something inside them was superior to
Circumstance
- Bruce Barton

Keep away from small people who try to belittle your ambitions.
Small people always do that, but the really great make you feel that you,
too, can become great.
- Mark Twain

DEALING WITH MY FIRST REAL SETBACK

I had been working at Salon Marc's for about six years, and was about 2 years into my laser business, in turn giving Marc a portion of the profits as 'rental space' in his spa. I had also moved into a tiny 500 square foot condo, my first home purchase that I had made with some help from my mother. My down payment was only about $5,000 and my mortgage under $1,000 and I'd decided after almost two years it was time to be on my own again. Living at my parents had served its purpose.

I had encountered a man at a mutual friend's house and he had proposed that we go into business together. This man and his brother seemed to have it all. They appeared to be very well off, had their heads screwed on straight and were very business oriented. I felt like these two men had opened my eyes for the very first time in my life to the possibility of going completely solo and becoming my own boss and the owner of a very large and profitable spa. Our mutual friend, Anthony vouched for them as the two brothers were dealing with many properties that Anthony and his wife were also investing in.

This automatically made me comfortable with the brothers and the decision to move forward with the proposed partnership. After all, they had the same idea as me; they wanted to build a large and luxurious medical spa located in the heart of downtown Toronto, and we would split the profits. They sold me the idea impeccably and I fell hook, line, and sinker.

I told my boss Marc about the offer and about how I was thinking about striking out on my own and he had given me the thumbs up to pursue my dream. I continued to work at the spa, as I needed to continue to perform laser treatments to pay those $10,000/month bills while venturing out with my new found friends Scorpio and Raphael in this new business idea. I was meeting all my obligations at work at this point and spending countless hours driving back and forth, sometimes multiple times daily, meeting with the two brothers. There was so much to do and I was more than happy to do it because in the distance dangled the hope that I would be my own boss, get my life on track, and stop living hand to mouth. I spent days upon days choosing our perfect, very large and very expensive location and developing our plan of opening a luxury spa in the downtown area.

Scorpio and Raphael had promised to fund the entire project and wanted my expertise and passion to help build and run the facility. It looked as if I had finally caught a break; it just seemed to be too good to be true. Now, I'm going to share with you a lesson that I think everyone needs to learn for themselves because until they experience it, they will never truly believe it - things that are too good to be true, usually are! Scorpio and Raphael wove a good tale. We had gone to Montreal to meet with spa designers; we consulted on the floor plan, the space needed for the treatment rooms, what the service menu would be, the décor; we ordered furniture, and pretty much did everything you would need to do to start a new business from scratch.

While the excitement and hope was intoxicating there was an inkling in my gut that told me that something wasn't quite right. Being so hopeful and excited at the prospect of running a business I pushed that little warning sign down as far as humanly possible. What set off my suspicions initially was that every single time I drove out to meet either of them for some business meeting or consultation, they would ask to borrow money, one hundred dollars here another hundred there for gas, for food, for whatever. At first, I didn't think twice about handing over my hard earned cash - even though I didn't have any to really give.

For people that gave off the impression of being high rollers they had a horrible habit of constantly forgetting their wallets and consistently asking me for money to cover expensive dinners, drinks, car rentals and more. You name it, I footed the bill for it and this really started to unnerve me. When we drove to Montreal for a consultation on the spa we had to rent a car that, naturally, went in my name. I was shocked to find out weeks later that they hadn't taken it back for over a month and that they left me with the four thousand dollar bill! I just couldn't believe it; they were supposed to be experienced businessmen. "Don't worry" they would say, "you'll get it back."

It was Scorpio who was mostly in the forefront and did most of the talking. You would believe anything this man was telling you if he was standing in front of you. He was likeable, and it is as though people like him find passion and courage in people and weave a web of deceit around it.

Scorpio had approached me, early on, needing $30,000 for a project development he had been doing that was near to closing. He asked me to approach Marc, since he had been a successful businessman for sometime, and Scorpio assumed he had the assets. Marc had met Scorpio, and had also liked him and found confidence in his persona and aura. When Marc was asked to borrow $30,000 for about 2 weeks, he almost flinched as this was something he had never done in his entire life - blindly lend someone so much money at one time. He looked me in the face and asked me if I trusted them, and I absolutely unequivocally said, "Yes. I promise you will get it back." I don't think there was ever any paperwork signed, just a gentleman's handshake agreement that Scorpio would return the funds immediately once he retrieved wherever it was originally supposed to come from, two weeks later.

I know you're thinking the worst. Strange how certain people come in your life, how certain people can make you do things you never thought you would do in a million years, and you really, can never say never. But Marc did get his money back, all of it, and it was this defining moment which secured my faith into the deal and into blind faith.

Things started to go in so many different directions that I didn't know what was what, what was real and what was an illusion or if it all was just a game. It was back and forth, hearing the little voices, believing in myself, believing in destiny, whatever would keep me pushing forward. I can't believe how stupid I was at the time not to see the signs but as they say hindsight is always 20/20. At certain points on the second trip to Montreal I began to hyperventilate. I would shake my head and wonder if this was for real or if I was making a mistake. But not even that gigantic red flag was enough to shake me from my delusional state of bliss and blind faith. All the distributors, the design companies we had met with and with whom we had placed orders were contacting me to ask where their deposit was, where and when they were to send the furniture and equipment

I had people pressuring me about when it was to be completed. My boyfriend Amir whom I was with for about 4 years at the time had not liked the business proposal at all. It actually turned out he didn't want me pursuing my dream, and didn't like that I wasn't available and was consistently working and devoting more attention to him as I had before. I felt like people were trying to put in their two cents and I felt like I wanted to focus so much and that I had not been able to; I started to break.

I was really destitute at the time and living on a really tight budget, and every time I took them out for an expensive dinner I was running the risk of losing my laser. One missed payment is all it can take sometimes.

Scorpio and Raphael seemed like an answer to my prayers; they built me up and then when I reached the top, they pushed me over the edge to plummet hard and fast to the bottom. After a few months had gone by and things were just not progressing the way I believed they should be I picked up the phone and called our mutual friend Anthony. It appeared that after talking to Anthony and his wife that they were having the same problems with Scorpio and Raphael that I was.

The two brothers were sending them on wild goose chases with investment properties. Anthony was a top-selling real estate agent and had placed quite a few offers for the brothers on many houses - but not one single deal ever went through to completion. Being in real estate, a business that relied on reputation, this lack of follow through could have serious consequences. Anthony had been going through the same disbelief and dilemma as I was myself. He had believed in them so much that he, personally, was spending thousands upon thousands of dollars on renovations on his own property thinking that the brothers were going to purchase all the offers of the several properties he had been showing them. However, Anthony, like me, came to the conclusion that the only people who were actually spending any money in these business ventures were the two of us and Scorpio and Raphael were consistently sending us on a dead end dream street.

Like all good con men Scorpio sold me a dream. Actually, he sold me more than a dream. He sold me confidence, happiness, and hope. It was a time in my life where I can honestly say I felt the most elated and confident - in the beginning. I felt great, which is something that had been lacking in my life for a very, very long time. They had made me feel that my dreams were possible and that's an indescribable feeling to have after fighting so long and hard for everything.

A few months after I had first met the brothers, everything came crashing down. Anthony's wife called me late one day frantic and hysterical, telling me to run as fast and as far away as my feet could carry from the business venture and Scorpio and Raphael - they were con artists! It still puzzles me how one person could do this to another person and how I didn't see the signs. Some people need red flags, others a slap in the face; I apparently needed a brick to the head. At the time of my epiphany there had been other stories circulating of other people being conned by these men and that was when I realized that it was time to throw in the towel on this impossible dream. This was my life's ambition but sadly to them it was simply a game. I was devastated. The time, the money, and heart that I invested in the project left me in deeper debt, depressed and even more confused.

You may think that this could never happen to you and that only an idiot would miss so many signs but Scorpio and Raphael appeared to be legitimate initially. They claimed to have owned their own construction business and several other businesses and appeared to own many properties. You may ask yourself why I hadn't done my research properly if I planned to invest so much time and money into the venture, and well, there is no good answer for that question. I was simply caught up in the dream that they were offering and I wasn't the only one.

Initially there appeared to be movement on the project; the location we chose had been gutted out completely to prepare from scratch a high-end sleek medi-spa. It was a few thousand square feet and we had decided to build the spa on the main level. We even saw architects and design teams for the project and Scorpio and Raphael planned to build condominiums above the spa to help with the revenue and mortgage payments once it was purchased. I had taken spa business classes at that time, spent thousands of dollars on them, and really started believing in myself again especially after my relationship with my boyfriend that had really been dragging me down, only to be knocked down further and harder than I ever was before. My boyfriend Amir and I finally came to an end at that time, and all things that year were taking its toll on me and my vision was starting to wane.

This story, however reminds me of Kairos, the god of happiness, or god of a lucky moment, which comes once in a lifetime, giving a man an opportunity to catch him by the wisp of hair on his forehead.

Kairos is an ancient Greek word meaning the right or opportune moment (the supreme moment). The ancient Greeks had two words for time, chronos and kairos. While the former refers to chronological or sequential time, the latter signifies a time in between, a moment in time when something special happens. What the special something is depends on who is using the word. While chronos is quantitative, kairos has a qualitative nature.

Kairos was the youngest son of Zeus, and it is said that Kairos watches for the favourable moment when the scales are balanced – a moment of happiness. Kairos slips smoothly into your life if you are alert and dare to seize opportunity. Those who run away from problems, who are afraid to act and to change cannot catch Kairos and his lucky moment. Kairos gives a chance to the man, but only if the man chooses to act. If he takes action, he can succeed or not, but if he doesn't, he'll never catch that divine moment. Kairos provokes a man to do daring acts, to love, to sacrifice for the good of others.

One moment with Kairos in which we truly lived is more important than living a hundred years without it. In it, we come in touch with eternity.

MANAGING PERSONAL PRESSURE

Everyone I know always seems to have one area of their lives that just doesn't seem to match the success and standards of the others; they have money but are unhealthy, they have a great family life but fail in the money department. I seem to have a string of bad relationships behind me. The most destructive of these is the one I shared with Amir. Things were bad with Amir from the very start and in hindsight I have absolutely no idea why I put up with his menacing behaviour for so long. Amir and I dated for most of my time working at Salon Marc.

Having read more about the subject of abusive relationships since breaking up with Amir I learned that this sense of dependency of the abused on the abuser is quite common amongst women, especially if they have been with their partner for a substantial period of time. You simply become accustomed to the abusive behaviour; it becomes a 'normal' part of everyday life and a day without it leaves you feeling strange and like something is off.

Stupidly, I stayed with Amir for many years and over time I became numb to a lot of his abuse. Even though I was in a relationship with a man who meant the world to me I felt very lonely. I suppose that it's true what people say - you can be in a room filled with people and still feel lonely if you are not happy with yourself.

There is one incident that sticks in my mind in particular and I whenever I recall it I wonder why I didn't leave him then and there. Amir and I had decided to go to Mexico for a holiday. It was the first time I had been away to another country with a man and I was so happy because in my mind only serious couples go on holiday together - it was all very grown-up and exciting. Our holiday began wonderfully as all holidays do and we were both having a great time until one night while sitting at a beautiful restaurant at our resort, I found myself staring at a couple sitting in the corner of the restaurant a few tables down from where we were seated. They were in a relatively quiet part of the restaurant and the lights were turned down low. The whole atmosphere looked and felt very romantic.

As I looked across at them I recall thinking that Amir and I must have looked equally romantic and intimate. At that moment the waiter came over to our table with a sly smile on his face; he had noticed that I kept glancing over at the couple in the corner. His smile broadened and he leaned closer to us, "He's just proposed to her" he said in a quiet voice. I smiled back at the waiter and then at Amir. Who knew? Maybe Amir would ask the same question some time down the road. I let my mind wander for a few minutes, smiling inwardly at the thought of settling down one day with Amir and raising a family, maybe even buying a little house with a white picket fence and garden. More fool me. What happened next makes me cringe to this very day and not simply because of the cruelty that was involved in the moment but at how much of a non-person I was when I was with Amir.

Taking a hold of my face, Amir turned my head towards the happy couple in the corner and with his face pressed closely to mine he whispered, "That's never going to happen to you, do you understand? Never." He then proceeded to tell me that he had no intention of ever proposing to me and that I would never find anyone who would be stupid enough to marry. He continued to snarl abusive remarks at me throughout the rest of dinner and I being dumb and in love took it lying down. Not one word did I say to counter any of his remarks. I would like to think that I said nothing because I was in shock; I had no idea where these remarks were coming from and why he wanted to hurt me so badly but precedent has shown me that I probably said nothing because I so desperately wanted to be loved and in a relationship with someone. I cannot remember if I cried then but I certainly cried later.

Amir's abusiveness eventually started to take its toll on my work. It soon came to a point where I was doing hundreds and hundreds of girls' makeup applications and it no longer seemed special to me. I became an automaton. I could no longer feel the artistry on my work. My brush became simply a tool rather than a channel for my creativity. Everything was mechanical and sterile. My work was utterly devoid of the passion with which I used to be filled every time I worked on a customer.

BREAKDOWN

I was still working at Salon Marc and it was frustrating to have to walk back into the salon and admit defeat in front of Marc and the rest of my colleagues. I was struck by a deeper feeling of disillusionment than ever before after the collapse of my business venture and relationships. I really gave up one day and remember walking into the salon and asked someone for a cigarette. As I do not smoke that seemed really weird to everyone and they asked if I was okay. No I was not okay. I felt that I had gone through so much crap in my life even though I had always tried to be a good person in every situation. I had always been kind hearted and generous, quick to forgive and ready to love. Why was this happening to me? I had always done everything by the book; I had been faithful in every relationship I had ever been in. And yet I kept getting the book thrown back in my face, and my partners just kept cheating on me. I had been physically, financially, emotionally, mentally and verbally abused by relationships for years. No amount of goodness and kindness seemed to stem the flow of negativity that kept on coming my way.

Suddenly I decided that I had had enough. That is it, I thought, no more bending over backwards to guys who just want to talk down to me; no more playing the nice girl. I did not want to be the good one anymore. Why should I bother to play nice if no one else wanted to? If they could break the rules for their own personal gain, why couldn't I? I thought that there was no natural sense of justice left in the world. The bad succeed and the good fail. My moral compass had turned and I really was at a low point.

For almost a year I had felt that way but it was not the real me. I played up to the bad girl persona, and I was utterly drained of all the kindness I felt I could offer. I had wasted it on people who just wanted to hurt me in the end. It did not seem to matter how much love or energy I put into work and relationships, it all turned sour just the same. Feeling as low as I was, I could not see how being good and kind had helped me achieve anything. It was only much later when I realized how important it is to always be the best person you can be, no matter what life throws at you.

At the time, though, I was going crazy. I really did take up smoking, and I partied staying up late some nights with friends. Crazy I know. Especially for someone who makes a living making people look and feel beautiful about themselves. I knew I was living a lie, but I was in self-destruct mode. I became distant and distracted, disinterested in the world around me. I did not care about anything at all, and I was unhappy and miserable. I was so angry that I had invested so much of my self into so many projects that ended in failure.

I hated having to start again from the beginning just when I felt I had climbed the first few rungs of the ladder of success.

Deep down I knew I was still a good person. It felt like I was purging myself of failure; like I was exfoliating all the weakness and self-doubt I had inside me. Of course, acting this way only made me more uncertain and more aware of my shortcomings. I could only hide them for a short while behind a thin veneer of indifference. My friends and family knew better. When I look back at the person I was then, I am sad. But life had dealt me a tough hand to play, and I was laying my cards down the only way I knew how.

CHAPTER SEVEN

I am thankful to all those who said no to me. It's because of them I did it myself.
~ Albert Einstein

Life's challenges are not supposed to paralyze you; they're supposed to help you discover who you are.
- Bernice Johnson Reagon

THE LAST CHAPTER AT SALON MARC

Throughout the excitement of buying my own laser, moving back home, struggling and then letting the dust still settle from the Scorpio/Raphael escapade and my breakup, I was still working hard at the salon making sure that we were still winning new customers and offering the best service packages on the market. I was really beginning to carve out my role in the world and I felt like Salon Marc was my true professional home. We had built up an excellent team dynamic, and I thought I was heading onwards and upwards. Marc's plans for expanding the business had succeeded and I had played a key role in helping him to realize his dream. The future still seemed bright and full of hope.

And then everything changed suddenly. Marc fired our manager, one of his best friends for almost 20 years. It surprised us all, and I think we were all in disbelief that it had happened at first. After some time had gone by, he decided to hire a family member to take over the management position with no previous experience in the industry or management for that matter and right from the start, she started to rub people the wrong way.

This woman acted superior and not at all like any of us who had worked there for so long. Her aloof attitude was all pervasive and it quickly undermined our working culture. If this had been the extent of her influence, I might have been able to pull through and steer the company back in the right direction, but I noticed a change in Marc too.

I had decided after almost six years of employment to change the terms of my pay structure so that I was just earning commission, taking 60% of the revenue. I no longer had a fixed salary, but the reputation I had earned for myself over the preceding years ensured that I would be making good money. Or so the theory went, anyway. After a few weeks went by on my new pay structure, I realized I was being booked for appointments *last* every week. This meant that my colleagues, who were junior to me in terms of experience and length of service, were earning more commission than I was.

There were three aestheticians working at Salon Marc at the time: with seven years' experience at the salon, I was the most senior; next came Valerie with five years' under her belt; and finally Janet who had only been there for a few weeks. It turned out that Janet was told to fill out all the bookings first because she was on an hourly pay.

Why were they doing this? I had put so much time and effort and money into the business, I deserved to be paid more than the rest. I felt betrayed and disappointed. I had always respected Marc for his shrewd business acumen but I always harbored the notion that he placed a greater value of friendship and loyalty than the sterile figures of his spreadsheets.

But no, it was better for Salon Marc, better for his bottom line and better for his business if I was given fewer bookings. Me taking 60% was not doing him any favours.

Naturally, I was very upset at the way things were starting to shape up, especially since I was starting to feel like I had always driven the salon towards success. I was freshly hurt and disillusioned by the inevitable breakup with Amir and the finale with the dead-end dream street escapade. Up until the point I confronted them about how I felt, I was sure that they would understand. Perhaps they had made a mistake. Perhaps they simply overlooked me by accident or did not realize that I would not be able to earn any money.

But my hopes were quickly shattered when we sat down and talked through the situation. They told me that this was how it was going to be from now on. There would be no going back to a salary or hourly pay structure. I had wanted to earn only commission, so now I was earning commission. That was that as far as they were concerned. If I had known that switching to a commission based pay structure was going to leave me this exposed and vulnerable I never would have agreed to it.

All my dreams for the future changed. *Again*. How could I stay there any more? How could I afford to stay here any longer? I had helped to build that spa, literally from the ground up. The spa was a part of me. Hell, it was me! I could not possibly go back to sitting in a corner waiting for clients, after all these years, picking up the crumbs from the table and begging for more clients.

All those years clearly did not matter to Marc anymore. In desperation I clung on to the job for several months while I gathered my thoughts. I could not afford to leave straight away, principles or not. Without a full workload, the hours dragged on each day. Sometimes

I would even leave early and go home, only returning if there was work for me.

The worst part about all of this is that I was starting to feel really down about myself. Events always seem to conspire against you when you are feeling low. The constant struggle to fill my schedule meant that the few tasks I did have were done half-heartedly. I just did not care anymore. I was tired of putting so much of myself into something only to have it thrown back in my face. Why should I bother any longer? Why not just do the bare minimum? Everyone else seemed to be doing just fine dragging themselves along at walking pace.

It got so bad that final year that I even broke one of my cardinal rules: never call in sick unless you really are ill. Some of the staff at Salon Marc were pretty notorious for taking days off work because they were 'ill'. It worked like clockwork for some of them. Even Marc would take a few days off now and again. I could probably count on one hand the number of times I had been ill and had to take the day off from my entire employment there. But once I got into that downward spiral of self-doubt, anger and resentment, I started to take days off here and there. I could not stand being in the spa knowing that all my efforts had been for nothing.

After months of neglect and discrimination at work, a car accident changed everything. Around Christmastime, I had been driving in a car with a girlfriend when we were rear ended very hard. Her car was totaled and we were both in severe shock, not to mention considerable pain. As you might expect, I called in sick for a couple of days after that and spent some time in hospital. When I called the spa on the second day of my convalescence I got a call back from the receptionist with a message from Marc: "Don't bother coming back."

"*Don't bother coming back?*" The receptionist had to repeat the message from Marc several times before it finally sank in. I had just been fired! Over the phone! He didn't even have the courage do it himself. I had hardly exploited the sick leave to which we were all entitled, and the car accident was a perfectly legitimate reason not to be at work. I had not called in sick more than five times over the course of seven years' dedicated service and hard work. Seven years! And all I got was a phone call!

That very same day, the receptionist and the new manager drove my laser to my condo. They would not even allow me to drive to the salon to collect my belongings. It was as though I did not exist anymore. They purged the salon of every trace of me, wiped their hands and dumped my $200,000 laser right on my doorstep.

I had no idea where I was going to work now, and I had no idea what would happen to my clients. More worryingly, I was not going to be able to pay the $10,000 + month in leasing fees and expenses. This could not be happening to me; it did not seem real. Once news of my sacking spread around the spa, the other girls started to worry about the security of their own positions. If this could happen to me, it could happen to them, too. No one felt safe. Marc had completely undermined their trust in him and in an instant, lost Salon Marc's most precious asset - its team spirit.

This was the moment in my life I knew for certain that I would never work for anyone else ever again. To have my hopes and dreams dangle for someone to quickly wipe it away clean was devastating. Leaving me vulnerable with someone else in control, wondering how I was going to eat and put food on the table was a time that I'll never forget. Never mind the lease payments I had to figure out how I was going to pay for the roof over my head.

Marc was not just my boss, he was my friend, my mentor, my father figure, everything really. As a gay man he had an easy and carefree way around me and around other women. It was easy to be around him. I knew that he could see me as person not just a physical conquest. He valued me and respected me more than anyone else at the time. It felt comfortable to be around a man who didn't make any advances towards me, to just be friends of the opposite sex. We actually hung out together after work all the time, we had dinner together and we were really great friends; not just colleagues at work. He was a great male friend to have. He had his moments with difficult people like most of us, and when he made a break from someone, he certainly made sure that it was a clean break. There was no going back for him. I think that is what made this unhappy event all the more harrowing. I knew that he had cut me out of more than just his spa; he had cut me out of his life. Things just kept getting worse and worse.

Looking at the laser machine sitting in my tiny little living room, I vowed never to set foot into the spa building again; my feelings were hurt in a different way, not the same as a boyfriend breakup, it was almost as though my own family had disowned me. What had been the entire focus of my adult life was gone, and it was devastating.

BETRAYAL AND THE HOME SPA

Picking yourself up and dusting yourself down is easy advice to give, but when you have to do it yourself, it suddenly becomes much harder. One thing seemed clear to me now: if I wanted to succeed I was going to have to do it alone. Salon Marc had taught me a great deal and I knew I was good at my job. But where to start? How do I work for myself?

To begin with I did not have a huge amount of choice in the deciding how or where. I had a laser in my apartment so it stood to reason that I would have to start treating people in my own home.

I ended up treating clients in the living room of my teeny tiny one bedroom, 500 square foot condo on a fold-up massage table. When my customers occasionally asked why I was operating out of my own apartment, I found it hard to explain to them what had happened. It still hurt too much. I tried not to divulge too much personal information unless I was talking to a client I had been working with for years. I probably found their company as therapeutic as they found my treatments.

During the two years I worked out of my living room, I also developed a laser training course for students interested in the field. Recalling my own struggles when purchasing, and lack of guidance and direction, I wanted to help other young professionals starting out in the beauty industry. On top of this, I would stay up late for hours on the computer, perfecting my website and adding as much pertinent information I could, just as I had learned to do at Salon Marc.

After working from my home for some time, I wasn't able to make the client quota that I needed to keep up with my bills, and I became a few months behind in my laser lease payments. I was actually only a couple of months away from the end of my lease agreement, and at the end of it there would be a $20,000 dollar buyout, and I would finally own the equipment. This was the first time in my life that I asked for a dollar from anyone (other than a bank), and I hated it! But I had to ask. Sometimes shouldering a burden on your own is impossible and there is no choice but to ask for a helping hand and that is what I did no matter the bitter taste that it had left in my mouth. I had turned to my parents for help and I was desperate to do so.

I had no choice; if I didn't pay the five months lease payments that I was behind, which totaled at over $17,000, I was losing the laser - my livelihood. All those months and years, those clients, the grief and strife would be wasted and for nothing. I pleaded my case to them and explained my situation to them and they were happy to help after they realized how much debt I was in. They were shocked to see it come to this, and hadn't really realized how much of my expenses I actually had to keep up until I finally told them.

In hindsight, I really should not have moved out of my parents' house so prematurely when I first purchased the machine. My 500 square foot condo was a mansion to me because it represented freedom and financial independence but soon I was getting in over my head. Losing most of my clients from Salon Marc and not having a decent place to work greatly hindered my earning potential. However, despite leaving Salon Marc's I still had all of my laser client files. I could still call all of the clients that I provided laser service for but as far as the aesthetic clients went, the salon staff was told not to tell them where I had gone or how they could get in touch with me.

I sat down and calculated the revenue that I had earned Marc in advance for all the prepaid packages that had not yet been serviced in laser treatments and I totaled everything. I wrote down the clients' names, what they paid, how many treatments they had left and so on, and came to the calculation that Marc owed me $6000. These were treatments that I now had to perform in my tiny home so why should he get to keep all the profits if I wasn't serving the clients in his salon. Marc gave me the balance without hesitation and then when I asked for my severance pay he said that technically I was not an employee and that he did not have to give me anything at all. The communication between us two had been through the receptionist and we hadn't spoken after he fired me over the phone. Well he didn't even do that himself, he got the receptionist to do that too.

Marc said that I had only been technically on commission the last year that I was in his service. In his eyes this made me a contractor and if I was simply a contractor he was not entitled to pay me my seven weeks of severance pay (one week's pay for every year that I had worked at Salon Marc). I stood there shaking my head in disbelief with the phone in my hand about a man I used to hold so close to my heart, a man I had treated as family - and a man I hardly recognized anymore. After the conversation that day the receptionist as the mediator, I decided to take my claim to the Ministry of Labour and after explaining my situation and the events that had transpired between myself and Salon Marc, I was awarded my severance pay. I gave the leasing company the money that I had owed them and made subsequent monthly payments on the laser, dividing the $20,000 evenly over several months. I had won a personal victory and made the first small step towards success once again.

TAKE EVERY OPPORTUNITY THAT COMES YOUR WAY

Life is full of opportunities, even if sometimes we cannot see them clearly. They may not always be obvious, but they are always there if you look for them. In practice, this means that we should never burn our bridges. Try to keep our options open. If one course of action does not seem right today, it may be tomorrow, next week or even next year. Being kind and friendly to everyone you meet in a personal and professional capacity is a good way of ensuring that the contacts you make in life last forever. Who knows what the future holds? Who knows what opportunities any one of your friends or colleagues might bring your way?

If we treat everyone with courtesy and respect, like colleagues not enemies, we can forge lasting relationships with a wide network of peers and all draw on each other's experiences of life. It may not seem like it, but the world is full of people who want to help you. By maintaining a positive mental outlook you will gradually start to surround yourself with similarly positive people. We all feel down sometimes, but being negative can put a real strain on personal and professional relationships, so it is always important to appear to be positive even if you are feeling unsure of yourself. It is your 'game face'.

Of course, this is easier said than done, but these are all gradual processes. Take one step at a time. Avoid people who are themselves negative, or those who can only see problems and not solutions. Give those who say you cannot do something a wide berth and try to identify instead a positive role model who you admire and respect. They do not have to be a celebrity or a famous person from the dusty pages of history; instead, they can be a close friend or family member, perhaps even a colleague at work - your boss even! Draw strength from their successes. Look at how their attitude towards life has given them the strength and confidence to enjoy life to fullest.

But whoever you choose to look up to, remember that you are the one who is in control, and you are the one who will have to call all of the shots. Do not try to imitate your role models because we each have our own path to walk, and mirroring other people's successes will never lead to true self-fulfillment. Instead, look at how they approach everyday life. What drives them? How do they use this to make them happy? What can I learn from them?

BUILDING THE BUSINESS

I had taken the idea of traveling to doctor's offices

from my time working at Dr. Zara's and implemented the idea into my own business. I needed as much revenue to keep pushing forward and had to figure out along the way how I could do this while creating my program and working from home. I traveled to other spas and salons who wished to add the revenue of laser hair removal to their brochure without having the expense of buying the equipment themselves. I packed up my laser in my car and I drove everywhere. I needed to make money and I needed to make it fast as next month's payment creeps up on me quite quickly and I needed to make sure that I kept on the ball. Moving from spa to spa and hiring my laser out was one of the best business decisions that I could have made. I found great locations that we still service to this day. We book a 'laser day' at the location and try and book as many clients in as possible in that one day. While hiring my laser out I gained a valuable lesson that I use in my professional life - you can't always get what you want so you have to be flexible and explore other opportunities and happy mediums. These salons couldn't afford their own lasers at the time so they went to the next best thing. While I am sure that they would have preferred to own a laser and keep all the profits for themselves it was not an option at the time so they hired one from me. Be flexible in your approach to business and life - some benefits are better than no benefits.

I had up to eight or so other locations that I frequently visited; some were very busy and some were not so busy. The one constant was that I kept constant. I needed that laser beeping as much as possible! I even put together a laser rental program for other technicians who wanted to rent the machine and treat clients themselves in their own locations.

People would always ask why in the world I would hire out something so valuable and critical to my livelihood to someone I did not know from Adam. I would always tell these people that my renters were all good people; you get a feeling from people and I never once thought that any of my renters, and now colleagues would maliciously do something to my laser. They treated it with care and I knew that.

The best advice that I can give anyone just starting a new business or career, no matter what profession it is, is to get advice from those that have been in your field the longest but also those that have been in the field for a shorter period of time; you need the traditional and modern perspective so that you can mould the two into a fresh new approach to your business. I should also add that sometimes people that are not in your industry can have valuable insight into your business because they too have a different way of looking at things. Ask, and you will always find your answers.

MY FIRST LAWSUIT

I moved in with my new boyfriend Dean, into his condo, after I had spent almost 2 years operating my laser business out of my little condo. I was served with a lawsuit. It was the owners of the building where we were to build our dream spa in Toronto. The Scorpio and Raphael fiasco. I was being sued for $1.5 million, $750,000 personally and $750,000 against my business. "Take a deep breath," I thought, "*this isn't really happening.*"

Since the property and its insides had been completely gutted it was hard for the owners to resell the property. The value had obviously been depreciated and they lost revenue in rent every month. I think the monthly rent was about $8,000 in that location at the time, and I was being sued for months and months of rent, and leaving the building gutted. (The brothers in turn were being sued for the same.) The only thing was, it wasn't my signature on the dotted line it was Scorpio's, but it was still my business name they had put on the lease agreement. I actually felt sorry for the property owners at the time the events transpired, as they had also been a pawn and involved in deception.

I had been given a referral to a lawyer in Toronto and given him a retainer and the only money I had, an extra $3000 left over from the sale of my own condo, and thank the Lord I even had that to give to the lawyer. I have now learned a lot over the years about legal issues, things you don't obviously think about unless you are in the situation. There is a 2 year limitation on being served or suing someone personally, so one of the $750,000 lawsuits had to be dropped, as it was just over 2 years since we had started movement on the project. I was still however being sued for Laser Spa Group, my company and there is a 6 year limitation on initiating a lawsuit regarding commercial properties. Someone can legally sue you for 6 years of rent once you leave after you have signed a legal document. Well now my case is a little complex as we already know, but as they say, tell it to the judge.

I wasn't able to get a business loan or any financing of any kind as my credit was pulled, the $750,000 lien showed on my business. It was hard to expand and hard to grow during that time.

A few years went by with a little discussion here and there with my lawyer over the phone, several times via email and in person. It seemed the owners of the property really wanted to get the brothers, but had had failed attempts at finding them, and actually even serving them at all. The property owners a couple of years later notified me again, and wanted me to settle for $80,000 and they would drop the case against me.

Settle for what? I was still living hand to mouth and I was still making ends meet and pushing forward and pushing my dream, juggling my teaching, clients, rentals of the machine and trying to make things work out.

I'd been dealing with this lawsuit looming over my head for years, for the duration of my pregnancy and the eventual breakup with Matteo's father Dean, all the while trying to keep game face and run my business.

After four years of stresses and anxiety, they eventually dropped the lawsuit. They decided to dismiss and have signed a letter of release, relieving me of this long drawn out litigation. I knew in my heart it would end that way, the truth is the truth and it always comes out in the end. So many close calls, but you know what? We all have them. You just keep on going and have faith and know deep down that you will come out a winner.

I'm also now convinced that the only thing that kept me going with all those setbacks and years of hard knocks was never to lose faith, and that I actually loved what I did. You've got to find what you love, and that is true for your work as it is for your mates. Your work is going to fill a large part of your life, and the only way to be truly satisfied is do what you believe is great work. And the only way to do great work is to love what you do. If you haven't found it yet, keep looking, and please don't settle. As with all matters of the heart, you'll know when you find it. And, like any great relationship or career, it just gets better and better as the years roll on. So keep looking until you find what you love.

BOZANA

CHAPTER EIGHT

You can spend minutes, hours, days, weeks, even months over-analyzing a situation; trying to put the pieces together, justifying what could've, should've, would've, happened. Or you can just leave the pieces on the floor and move the fuck on.
-Tupac

In love, no one can harm anyone else; we are each of us responsible for our own feelings and cannot blame others for what we feel. That is the true experience of freedom: having the most important thing in the world without owning it.
- Maria in "Eleven Minutes"

LEARNING TO BE ON MY OWN

I have not been lucky in love. I've been blessed with some amazing moments over the years, but somehow have managed to choose partners who did not want what I wanted, did not feel what I felt, and did not want to walk beside me into a future together. I have really had to sit with this and try and figure out what part of this was my doing, and how to change it, or what to look for in a man, because I constantly chose a partner who was not walking with me. Not only was he not walking with me but he was subtly trying to kick my feet from under me every chance he got.

The only constants that have ever been there for me were my family members and I thank God for them each and every night. I cannot stress enough how important it was for me to hear my mother's words over and over again to become a stronger person and although she always gave the same lectures and tried to teach me the same life lessons they still meant the world to me. I actually never got enough of hearing it. I felt as though I needed it repeated to me as my heart would always take over my brain when it came to me falling in love. I was heartbroken a lot, and it took a very long time for me to heal my heart and start finally 'using my brains' as my mother would say.

I suppose that at times I was too stubborn for my own good and if it wasn't for my mother drilling me with the same old words of inspiration and lessons and my stepfather's constant never-ending words about how I should find a good man, work hard, be a good person, live a simple and happy life, use the knowledge and gifts God gave me, and learn to be alone for awhile to find myself instead of running into the next relationship, then I may not be the person that I am today and I may not be where I am today. I only wish that I had smartened up earlier because while I was going through the heartaches and the dramas I could sense my mother making herself sick over my misfortunes or for every broken heart I got. As a mother now I am certain I will give my son the same advice and hurt like hell if he gets hurt in any way. I couldn't even imagine seeing him in any pain, and I suppose we realize these important things and life lessons as we get older. We should have always listened to our parents from the beginning. And as the old saying goes; "Learn from other people's mistakes, you don't have time to make all of them yourself".

Why do we sometimes keep falling for the same person, and why can't some of us find solitude instead of sticking in a dead-end relationship? Often we fall in love with a person before we have fully gotten to know them. By this point it's too late—you've already stretched your heart for someone capable of bruising it. This is what love requires: vulnerability and trust. Hopes and expectations rise along with the awareness that it can slip away one day. What we can do is to at least live in the moment and love one another the best that we can. After being with one another for some time in a relationship, that perfect perception of the other person isn't so perfect anymore, and something may have changed or shifted. Sometimes we can recover from this, sometimes we can't. That is the one of the challenges of entering a new relationship.

For a long time I didn't believe I would find love so I subconsciously chose partners who I knew would be a challenge. I am no longer interested in this challenge. I told myself when my last relationship failed with my son's father, that I would never put myself in a situation where I didn't know where I stood in someone's life again; where I felt unsteady and unloved.

So, there's a moral here: People come into our lives to teach us something. People come and people go and people make a difference. And it's okay that they're not in our lives anymore. It feels weird to be imagining a future together one year and then well-wishing a few years later, but that's exactly how it's supposed to be. And I'm exactly where I'm supposed to be. We all are.

BOZANA

CHAPTER NINE

To laugh often & much; to win the respect of intelligent people & the affection of children; to earn the appreciation of honest critics & endure the betrayal of false friends; to appreciate beauty; to find the best in others; to leave the world a bit better, whether by a healthy child or garden patch, or redeemed social condition & know even one life has breathed easier because you have lived. This is to have succeeded.
- Ralph Waldo Emerson

You must know that in any moment a decision you make can change the course of your life forever: the very next person you stand behind in line or sit next to on an airplane, the very next phone call you make or receive, the very next movie you see or book you read or page you turn could be the one single thing that causes the floodgates to open, and all of the things that you've been waiting for to fall into place.
- Anthony Robbins

PREGNANCY SHINED THE LIGHT INSIDE ME AGAIN

Out of all the highs and lows of my life to date, nothing has been more important than the birth of my son Matteo. Everything else seems to fade into insignificance when I think about him and all the happiness he has brought me. Becoming a mother was the greatest gift of my life. If I were not a mother I would find meaning and purpose in some other way, but being the mother of a remarkable little boy gives me a sense of wholeness, great meaning, and satisfaction.

It was during the Salon Marc drama that I met and started dating a man named Dean. Although I was instantly attracted to Dean and his bad boy persona, I never dreamed that I would end up carrying his child. But that's jumping ahead of myself a little.

I started dating Dean a couple of years prior to us getting pregnant. Up until this point I had still been working hard out of my own condo. Dean and I found a great place where I could set a room aside for work and we quickly moved in together. It was a perfect set up. I was living with the man I loved and I could continue to operate my laser from our new apartment. It was all fine as long as it was the two of us.

The thing is though, we had asked for a baby. We really wanted to bring a new life into the world and had tried to get pregnant for a few months. As it turned out, we both remember the exact night we conceived. It was so strange. It was as though God had answered our prayers and graced us with the most beautiful boy in the world.

I loved every minute of being pregnant. Once again I felt like I was moving forward with my life. I was in my thirties and ready to be a mother. The life that was growing inside me filled me with deep senses of satisfaction and anticipation at the same time. It was such a new experience to be carrying inside of me the potential for a whole new person. I could hardly wait to give birth, so I embraced the whole thing completely. I was going to be a mommy!

When I think about my relationship with Dean, this was the one time when God had truly heard our prayers and given us what we had asked for. Things between us had been a bit tense but we still loved each other and we both really wanted to have a son, and the moment I found out that I was pregnant we both knew with certainty that we would have a beautiful little boy and he would be everything we had asked for and dreamed of.

While I was pregnant I read several books, as most women do, about being pregnant and even listened to several audiotapes about the whole process. It was around this time that things started to break down between Dean and me. I tried to stay positive throughout these rough patches. Even though our son had not been born yet, I did not want to surround him with negative experiences. So I used to sing to him in the car as we drove along. I knew he could hear me inside, and I knew it would make him happy.

Dean and I were just not getting on well anymore. He and I had just been in this relationship with too much bitterness, and there was too much negativity almost on a daily basis. Despite my best efforts to put on a brave face, and pretend for so long that things between us would get better, it started to take its toll on me. Just like with Amir, I found myself in a relationship thinking that if I loved someone hard enough and with enough conviction, they would change for me and love me back just as much. Once again I found myself in a destructive relationship, only this time I was pregnant. Even so, we stuck together throughout my pregnancy. The thought of my son made me so happy that I felt strong enough to put up with the negativity.

Nine months after I conceived my waiting was over, and I went into labour. I had a really rough delivery with the baby. My water had broken at about 10am on October 4th, but it was not until 7:30am the following day, October 5th that I finally gave birth. I was in full labour for about 20 hours and let me tell you it was the most excruciating time of my life. My labour was very hard and very long. Dean stayed with me the entire time and tried to be very supportive. I was given three epidurals, (yes 3!) and none of them seemed to take effect.

After hours of pushing my son Matteo came into

the world blue in the face, he was taken away from me seconds after he came into the world. He was struggling to breath and he swallowed his meconium and they had rushed him to NICU (Neo-Natal Intensive Care Unit). I remember the nurse saying there was an 80% chance he would be OK.

It was hard going through all that chaos and commotion and not knowing what was going to happen. I was surrounded by hustle and bustle and commotion all the time, but no one gave me any news about my baby. My mind was reeling. There were so many different faces coming in and out of my room that I could hardly keep track of who was actually meant to be caring for me. Staff shifts would start and finish and all the while I would lie in bed hoping for some news. An anxious face would sometimes lean over me and check that I was still OK and I would try to find out about my son, but all I would get was a non-committal smile as if to say just relax. You need to recover. Don't worry about anything but getting better. Save your strength. We were all finally able to see Matteo in a little incubator and I was asked to pump some milk for him. I visited him there over the next few days and didn't know when he would be able to come to my room, and when we would be able to go home together.

I remember the nurses finally bringing him to my

room instead of staying in the NICU as a four day old baby crying for his mother. Since I was in the maternity ward I was constantly surrounded by crying babies, somehow I knew the sound of my baby's voice and I knew he was finally coming to stay with me in my room. The nurses had not told me that they were going to bring him to me that day, but I knew he was coming as soon as I heard him cry.

It was the happiest moment in my life. How did I know? It felt so natural and so spiritual and so real. It was the proudest moment of my life, and I knew good things were coming.

I decided to name him after my dad Mate, whom I loved dearly. But since my son was a new person, I wanted to give him a new name too. So we gave the name a bit of a twist. We called him Matteo. This way my dad is always with me.

After Matteo was born, things with Dean did not really change much for the better. I was still in a relationship with a man who could not love me like I loved him and the mental anguish over many reasons had taken its toll. Matteo had not changed that. Finally I decided to end the relationship when my son was a few months old. I did not deserve this and neither did Matteo. My relationship with Dean seemed to be an endless circle of negativity and I could not take it anymore.

I was left paying the rent on my own with a young child. I stayed in our home for a few more months until I found something a little more affordable. This was just like a divorce - a different breakup than the others and I had my son to take care of as well as myself and my business. Alone.

I ended the relationship and have since settled happily with my son. I had fallen in love with Matteo and did not want him to see anything but good in his life. We are both now in a good place where we can give him that, and Dean is a wonderful father to Matteo and loves him so much I know that for certain.

My career has always been my survival guide and my saving grace from all of life's turmoils, failed relationships and all the ups and downs. It was the one thing that I had continued desire and love for, and it was so rewarding giving myself completely to something and having it as a constant in my life, and now I had my son too. I always yearned to learn; when I was finished with something, mastering it, I wanted to move on to the next idea. I had something to funnel my energy to. I was never lost in that direction and always felt content in fitting right in being a medical aesthetician and service provider.

I have wondered at times where I would be if I had found someone who wasn't such a firecracker, was manic in some way or didn't care about the next pretty girl that came his way. Someone who was successful, loyal, respectful and who I could also learn from and be my mentor would have been such an easier ride along the way.

Don't think that if you are a good mother though, that you will be happy. Be happy and you will be good at everything that is meaningful and valuable in your life. Raising a child to become a good person is a most honourable goal, and attaining it begins with a mother's own inner transformation. This inner transformation happens with solitude sometimes.

CHAPTER TEN

I believe that everything happens for a reason. People change so that you can learn to let go, things go wrong so that you appreciate them when they're right, you believe lies so you eventually learn to trust no one but yourself, and sometimes good things fall apart so better things can fall together.
- Marilyn Monroe

Once, someone asked me what pleasure I took in riding for so long. 'Pleasure?' I said. 'I don't understand the question.' I didn't do it for pleasure, I did it for pain.
- Lance Armstrong; Winner Tour De France 1999 – 2006

FLYING SOLO -
MY PROGRAM AND MY
VISION FOR THE FUTURE

People always ask me if I ever feel that I limited myself in the beginning by focusing on laser hair removal and my answer is always the same - No! Laser hair removal in the thirty or so years since its inception is still the number one non-surgical cosmetic procedure being performed by aestheticians and physicians alike and, thankfully for me and countless others in my shoes, the market is still booming. People are spending millions of dollars every year on hair removal and this is not going to stop; the media and Hollywood play a critical role in this and thankfully I do not see them endorsing overly hairy chested men or leg hair on women any time soon.

I may not seem very modest but that is because I truly am good at what I do and I worked hard to become good at what I do. My current path is to instill my skill and my work ethic into every one that I teach. There are several different programs and institutes currently out there. If these girls do not learn from me, they are going to learn from someone else, and my hope is they choose someone who knows what they are doing, someone who is passionate about their work, and someone who can relate to them.

The training courses that I designed have been a natural progression to my business, a business that I want to make even bigger and stronger than it is now. My vision for the future is to have a full cosmetic institute offering full aesthetics and full medical aesthetics, much more equipment and a bigger facility, a full curriculum of both aesthetics and medical aesthetics in a beautiful institute. I want to educate people; it is something that I am quite passionate about and something that I truly enjoy doing. You should always follow your joy, no matter how difficult it may seem to do. I do not want these women to just go out, buy a machine and not feel comfortable using it; I want them to know what it is they are getting into and to feel comfortable providing these services to other people in a professional setting. My program ensures that they will be able to do this and if for some reason they do not feel comfortable or choose not to go into the profession soon after graduating then I am there for them. My students are always welcome to come back for a refresher course to get their confidence back if they've lost it or simply to build it up even more.

What I remember most about working in Dr. Zara's office is the time that I spent watching the nurse. I was with her for nearly three months before I was left on my own. Hearing the consultation over and over again, seeing the treatments, the different body parts, the angles, how to position the equipment, the patient, what to say, what not to say, who to treat, and who not to treat - it was all so overwhelming at times. There was and still is so much to learn. While I learned many, many things that I use to this day about how I should carry on my business from this nurse I was also fortunate enough to learn some things that I should not do.

The most important of these "don't" lessons was to remember where I started out and how I felt while I was starting out. I feel that bosses and the people that own businesses need to remember that they were in the beginner's shoes one day not so long ago - the worker, the student, the rookie, the apprentice with wide eyes and wonder wanting to learn every single thing there is to know about what they are about to do and the path that they are about to embark on. Most times when you become a master of your craft you tend lose sight of who you are teaching and what it was like to be in the shoes of a student and forget that. When you are teaching some bright-eyed and bushy tailed young student, they are scared and look at you as if you are talking in a completely alien language. Teaching for me is finding the well balanced and happy medium where my students learn the theory and background of lasers, the appropriate bedside manner, and how to put the two components together and actually perform the treatments that are being asked of them effectively and with a positive attitude. My students always enjoy the classes that I have designed for them no matter their age or walk of life. My students want to do something new with their lives, and what a great career to start after only a few of weeks training. It's a great starting path to becoming an entrepreneur for so many women. I had even helped girlfriends wanting to start their own clinics over the years with my advice and as a sounding board. I never kept what I knew to myself. I have freely given my knowledge and my hands-on insight because I care about them, and about wanting to make it in this big world as a woman. Women want to own their own home, own their own business and survive on their own. This program and profession gives women the opportunity to step into a great environment and to feel good about themselves too. You can take the original Mary Kay philosophy and run with it. She has empowered thousands of women to start businesses of their own. She was well loved and wanted everyone to have a piece of the pie.

An important and hard earned lesson that I learned very early on in my career as a business owner is that I want to encourage other young women to follow their dreams when they are in a position of power and teaching someone else. Often in my career I have come across bosses who felt intimidated by one's desire to strike out on their own. I never understood how people like this operated; how do you spend years with someone, get to know their dreams and desires and who they are as a person and then turn around and punish this person, who you've worked beside day after day for years, for wanting to go out there and fulfill their dreams? I made a vow to myself that this would never be me. They may have forgotten that they were in rookie's shoes one day and forgotten that they needed encouragement, help, and advice. I'm going to encourage and help the girls that I teach and work with because I believe that if you help everyone and are kind to everyone that one day, when you need it most, they may be in a position to help you and they will return the favour.

Know which bridges to burn and which hands to hold. Instead of knocking someone down who might be competition for you, try saying good luck for a change. I have never feared competition from my staff or students not because I think that they are not good enough, I would not have hired them and kept them on as employees if they didn't know what they were doing but because it takes serious time and effort to build a business.

To make it big in this business as in every other business you need good instincts, you need to know how and when to take risks and you need an incredible support system. There is a business out there for everyone who works hard and wants it bad enough and that's something that I tell everyone including my colleagues and students. As long as you are the best that you can be and you don't tarnish your image or your name, because it's what you will have and be the rest of your life, you will succeed.

I still have students texting me, emailing me questions, or occasionally asking for advice and I always answer all of their questions and try to help them in what ever way that I can. It is my responsibility still to help them and if I don't then that means that I never cared about them or my work from the beginning and in a way that would make me worse than the owner who fired his protégé.

DIVERSIFYING TO EXPAND THE POSSIBILITIES - BECOMING A LASER INSTRUCTOR

During my pregnancy and a few months before Matteo was born, I could no longer sustain my business operations in our condo. There simply was not the space. After looking around the neighbourhood, I found a small place with a hair salon above it. It felt like oddly familiar territory, so I took the basement and set up shop. It was not ideal, by any means but it gave me all the space I needed and I could walk there from our apartment. Since I was self-employed I started working out of my new studio three weeks after I had delivered Matteo (and a couple of days before I gave birth). Not full-time shifts after the pregnancy, mind you, but a couple of hours a day to treat clients that had purchased packages and needed to be on schedule for treatments, and we also needed the income. During my pregnancy, however, I brought my curriculum to a very well established aesthetics school very close to our home, and started to finally teach others my forte.

I had taken a job as laser instructor for the duration of my pregnancy and sometime thereafter. I had approached the school a few times over the course of 3 years, as that was one of the only schools that hadn't had a laser course and I wanted to offer the one I had developed. I researched online, and focused on putting together a great overview, template and manual for a student wishing to get into the lucrative and exciting career. They had accepted my offer, but I wasn't getting the commission I had wanted. Since it was my work, my laser and my knowledge on the table I felt I deserved more, but I was grateful for the opportunity to start another advancement in my career, teaching others what I had known now for years and felt so completely knowledgeable and comfortable. The Ministry of Education recognizes an instructor with at least 4 years continued practical experience in their profession such as a hairdresser or aesthetician as equivalent to their standards in being able to teach in that craft. I hadn't gone to teacher's college, but I did have 5 or so years' experience strictly performing laser treatments at the time of my hiring. The ministry also has certain guidelines about hours of instruction, and programs under 40 hours aren't fully recognized. Our new laser program fit the template. As most of the others being taught had fallen under the same guidelines.

I was now able to see how it feels like to stand in

front of a room with 10 - 15 plus girls at any given time and explain to them both theory and hands-on techniques for laser hair removal. The entire process takes up about 30 or so hours of lecture including an overview of how lasers and IPLs work, the physics of both lasers and IPLs, safety and efficacy issues, as well as hands-on practical experience. (IPL is an acronym for Intense Pulsed Light, just as LASER an acronym for Light Amplification by the Stimulated Emission of Radiation).

We discussed the most commonly used dermatologic lasers and their parameters and did a detailed overview of skin and hair. The parameters for permanent hair reduction were discussed and also presented. The lectures included laser and skin interaction, skin typing, operational and treatment safety measures. We discussed the management and treatment of adverse events and during our hands-on experience, also the benefits, expected results and outcomes, and available alternative treatments. My one main focus was on patient consultation, selection and education, contraindications and precautions. I made sure my students knew that consultation book inside out and how to effectively conduct a consultation to ensure the client or patient was comfortable with you as the operator and also with the treatment itself. Making eye contact and putting your own words into the book ensured your client was comfortable in your knowledge, and in turn booked their treatment.

I had taken what I was perhaps missing myself when I attended aesthetics school and tried to ensure they were happy with me as an instructor and also excited with the career itself. They all had been, and I had taught several girls by the end of my contract and was proud to see what I had helped create new ideas and visions, and also teach the girls a great profession. Most of them wished they had just taken the laser program as opposed to the aesthetics, as this was the exact field that suited them. I feel it is great to have both; the more knowledge you have in this industry the better. You will forever keep learning and forever keep taking classes. The program I created was also open to students not already enrolled in the aesthetics program, and we had made a consecutive 6 day program to accommodate mature students.

The school had decided some time later to change the hours of the program and how the curriculum was delivered. They wanted the laser course to be the very first class to be taught prior to any aesthetics treatments. This now new fresh class in front of me was looking at me the first day of school in disbelief and fear without having even touched a nail file.

I didn't like the changes, and didn't like the fact that now my course being started at the very beginning of their 9 month program. I was then asked to come back weekly or more often after the initial course to keep the students 'fresh in what they learned' until the end of the 9 months. Now, I was expected to physically come back, bring my laser and not have the use of it at my own place of business below the little hair salon near our condo.

I felt I needed to be compensated along with these new terms to our agreement. I was renting an IPL machine and a microdermabrasion machine for over $400 per day and bringing them to the school so the girls had more equipment to work on. This meant more cash out of my pocket as well.

I outlined the new revenue with all the students I taught and divided it by the actual hours I worked, plus my overhead and it came out that I would actually be paying *them* to work by the end of this new 'idea'. Since I was renting additional equipment to ensure everyone was having a hands-on experience, with two students on each machine and if there wasn't a student doing practical, they were practicing consultations and I was adamant on them having the perfect consultation. My website presence and online content was bringing in students for the school that never would have attended before, at over $3,000 per person. Again I felt back to not being in control and using my talents, intellect and hard work to benefit others. It just didn't make sense for me to stay and I clearly outlined in my proposal, what revenue I had generated for all of us collectively and what I needed to stay as an employee.

The owners of the school didn't see things my way, and it was ok. There were no hard feelings and we went our separate ways. I decided to take my new found experience as a laser instructor and implement that into my own business. I could still take students via my website and word of mouth, and make 100% of the revenue instead of a small portion. As I was already a customer for years because I owned their laser, I was able to send my new students to Clarion the distributor of the LightSheer post-certification and have the students certified through them as well. As a laser operator, to obtain malpractice and liability insurance, you need certification from a private career college, or from the distributor of the laser you are operating with. I was able to have the students first learn the craft, then they were able to work for themselves with a laser rental program I had in place. They were then able to get their insurance that they obviously needed post-certification. I found a beautiful private career college with a fully equipped theory room and treatment beds who taught mostly massage therapy, and they were willing to rent me space as needed. It was great.

I remember all the girls I have taught thus far and had always felt welcomed by them. At the beginning of every course, I see the fear and excitement at the same time in their eyes and I enjoy knowing that by the end of the program, the exam will be easy for them. I fine-tuned and honed my skills class after class after class. I implemented what worked, left out what did not work and knew that the one main critical piece of the pie was hands-on experience.

I tried to make sure I got every different body part for them to practice on, every single skin type from the fair-skinned ladies of the British Isles and Scandinavia to the women of darker skin from the Caribbean, South East Asia, and Africa so that they could treat everyone with confidence. I tried to give them pep talks and gave them as much advice, feedback, support, and scenarios as I could, to troubleshoot and try to stress the most important aspects. I wanted them all to know that I cared about their successes too, and I want students that have been taught by me to go out and feel confident enough in getting a job and hopefully the clinics, spas and salons that asked where they got their training would know that they had been in good hands.

CHAPTER ELEVEN

Everything will work out all right in the end. If it's not all right now, it's not the end yet.
- Unknown

The most beautiful people we have known are those who have known defeat, known suffering, known struggle, known loss, and have found their way out of the depths. These persons have an appreciation, a sensitivity, and an understanding of life that fills them with compassion, gentleness, and a deep loving concern. Beautiful people do not just happen.
- Elisabeth Kubler-Ross

MAKING A NAME FOR MYSELF

Things were looking up now and my work was gathering its own momentum. I remember clearly after Matteo was born having to bring my breast pump to work for months so that I could pump in between client appointments!

I realized pretty quickly that I could not afford to be a one-woman show anymore. My business was picking up quickly and I did not have the time to do all of the things that needed to be done. I had created the company Laser Spa Group for a reason, and I had a clear vision of a successful company thriving over the coming years. With a bit of luck I hoped I would be able to exploit franchising opportunities in the future. Things could move fast if I wanted them to, I just needed another pair of hands.

I had built up years of good rapport with all my clients, but I could not be in two places at once. I knew that I would have to hire an assistant and hand over my trusted customers to their care.

Many of them had pre-paid packages and needed to be treated, so I could not go back to having fewer customers. I was committed to them. I decided that I would hire an assistant that I trusted and I would start delegating the running of the business to them. They could take over some of my clients, provide the service packages I had developed and give me more time to spend with Matteo.

I found the perfect fit in Silvana, who had taken the laser course at the school I had first taught at. It was hard to let go of the day to day running of the business, but it was an important step for me. I learned to trust other people again. This meant that I only needed to worry about my strategic vision for the company rather than the smaller, but no less important, tasks. But of course, Matteo was also my real priority now.

Silvana had stood out from all the rest, and I knew I found someone that was trustworthy, loyal and a really hard-working young lady. She always asked to help bring the laser to my car, was polite and always went the extra mile for me at the school. I took the time to really teach her everything I knew and she had shadowed me for months, like I did years back at Dr Zara's so she would be confident enough to take on the clients that may be hesitant on having another technician service them. Funny thing is now they ask for her. She's been with me well over 3 years and hasn't called in sick once. My assistant has been one of those people in my life who I can say I'm blessed to have met and really enjoy working with. She can read my mind and I don't have to tell her twice to do something; it's already done and efficiently so.

At last I could also finally let go of the whole ideal relationship thing that had been plaguing me for years. Now that Matteo was born I had someone else to worry about and care for other than myself. It was the first time I truly felt okay being alone. Perhaps my greatest problem in the past had simply been my constant need to be in a relationship. Every time one ended, I looked for the next one to begin. I never gave myself time to think about me. By looking for love so hard, I cheated myself out of truly falling in love. Love finds you, you can't find love. Now that I had a son to love everything was different. You know, it is true what they say about true love. You do not know true love until you have a child.

I felt blessed and so happy I could finally give my love to someone that wanted it, and to someone who would give it back to me unconditionally. It was a complete circle of love and there was nothing else I needed. Matteo helped me to grow, to be strong and not be afraid to be alone. As I looked into his tiny face I just hoped that I would be able to raise him without exposing him to the growing bitterness that grew between Dean and myself during our relationship.

I had to focus on being a good mother and a good boss at the same time. I had two people to look after now, and balancing my personal and professional life was fast becoming an increasingly difficult act.

I love Matteo more than anything and only want him to see good in his life. Dean and I live separately but Matteo sees us both. He lives with me, and I never give Dean a hard time when he wants to see him. Some fathers don't want to see their children or be a part of their lives and that's terrible. I want the best for Matteo and I will do everything I can to ensure that he is always happy. I will protect him and love him forever.

LOOKING FOR LOCATIONS

One of the things that I am proud of is that I've kept in touch with past friends and colleagues and not burned bridges. My first aesthetics instructor, Zoe, and I remain friends and colleagues to this day and it feels truly great to have someone in my life who's been there since the very beginning of my career. Zoe is a wonderfully positive person. She's always happy, cheerful and accommodating for anyone. Entering her spa you feel welcomed, important and well taken care of. I look up to her and try to keep as positive an attitude as hers. Zoe is one of the reasons why I believe that you should keep in touch with all your old friends and colleagues. When my lease expired on my basement "spa" and I had nowhere to offer laser treatments for what would turn out to be six months, Zoe was kind enough to allow Silvana and I to use her facilities. For as long as I breathe I will never forget the kindness and friendship that Zoe bestowed on me in my time of need; it truly takes a great person to help another in the same line of work as them and not worry about the consequences that their success will have on your business.

Zoe helped me get back on my feet after my lease ran out, and was one of the locations that occasionally rented my services from the beginning after being let go from Salon Marc. She is a great friend and I am sure that she wouldn't have minded how long I stayed but I didn't want to risk overstaying my welcome.

After some time, it bugged me as the months went by not knowing where our new place of work was going to be. I yearned for a little spa to call my own. We had started to gain momentum in the business and we needed a bigger facility and fast. I wanted my own set of keys that wasn't in the basement, not in my apartment, or a friend's spa, but a real location that had a front door entrance to it.

I found a place that wasn't too far from Salon Marc. It had served as a salon and spa for years, and was up for lease. I thought the location would be ideal, and hoped I could find some of my old clients while in the neighborhood. It needed a lot of work, wasn't new but again I see the potential in everything and jumped at the chance. I had negotiated to purchase the location with the hopes of living in part of the building and running the spa in the other half. Dean and I had separated so I was also frantic to find a new home, as well as new place of business.

The landlady backed out of my proposal to purchase, which we had been discussing for a few months and she didn't want to sell the commercial property for the appraised value of which we had originally agreed on. It was Christmastime and I remember still being confused about the future and decided to call our mutual lawyer and ask him to then draw up a lease agreement, and I signed it. If she didn't want to sell then I thought leasing was the alternative.

After reviewing the leasing agreement at home over that Christmas weekend however, I realized what my bills would be with taxes, lease and renovations and I backed out. A friend told me that there is something called 'buyer's remorse' and there is a small waiting period when you can back out of a deal or lease. I realized later I was wrong, and it only applies to personal property not commercial.

The law office was closed for a few days for the holidays, and I wanted to be sure the keys and my letter got to them first thing when they opened. I mailed a letter, apologizing for my misjudgment. I said that I had been going through personal issues (which I was) and couldn't take the property. I couldn't afford it, with my son being my priority as well a single mother now. The property had been empty for almost a year prior to me wanting to take possession anyway. I thought the landlady would understand.

Well she didn't. Exactly a year later on the following Christmas Eve, I was served with papers. *Again.* She wanted $20,000. I remember being embarrassed in front of my mother and other clients who had been at our now new location getting services, and myself in the treatment room trying to figure out why the past was haunting me and why people wouldn't just leave me alone.

I didn't show I was upset, just realized it was something else that needed to be dealt with and I now had to put on my game face. Even when you are going through strife and difficulties, your game face is what you need sometimes in order to survive. Other people sometimes don't want to hear your dilemmas or dramas. Your family and friends do, but there might come a time when you may sound like a broken record and another 'here we go again'. I held a lot of the misfortunate situations that had happened to me over the years to myself most of the time. You don't want to be labeled as someone that doesn't know how to handle things and forever be the sad face in the room. We are all going through something in life and I think we need to be sensitive for everyone that comes in our lives. But you know the ones I'm talking about when I say some people always have something negative to say. They always have a headache or they always seem a bit down and say negative things to try deflate your happiness. They leave you feeling guilty or stressed out, down to your very last molecule. Some people bring unexpected lightness and comfort to your life and practically electrify you with their presence. People run away from energy vampires. Others gravitate towards happy souls. If you are feeling happy then inevitably you will make others around you feel happy too. People gravitate towards people that make them feel good. This human hardwiring keeps us alive. Sometimes a little pain will result in greater pleasure over the long-term.

Many of our peers and colleagues are aware of the conscious effort required to stay on top of your game. From the basics of rest, good nutrition and meditation and having a spiritual discipline, these are strategies that reflect those practiced by the most highly functioning professionals in our society.

It's game time - how readily can you put your game face on if you haven't devoted yourself diligently to your mental preparation as to your physical game? Even if there are barriers in the way. Look around you and you will readily find the elders, mentors or role models in your profession who have not just survived but prospered. Ask them what you need to do to ensure you are at your very best for as long as possible.

I went to see our mutual lawyer to discuss our options and we agreed to a settlement of $7,000, which I paid monthly for 7 months. Be careful what you sign, be careful who you into business with and be careful that others think as you do. Learn from your instincts so you don't have to make the same mistakes twice. I should have listened to my instincts and waited for the right spot, instead of taking something that didn't feel 100% right, especially since the original deal to purchase fell through. I rushed, and yes I paid for it.

HOME SWEET HOME

Without much further looking, I met the owners of a well-established salon, Salon Michele, who had been in business over 30 years. I had actually known them almost my whole life, as they had cut my hair when I was in high school. It felt great that we had known each other and had an understanding and respect for one another. I was able to run my business my way, and pay them rent in doing so. I was getting a great location, beautiful building with great parking and room to expand. Finally Silvana and I had front door entrance and Laser Spa Group was just about to get rolling.

Having been there well over 3 years now, this is likely to be one of the most rewarding years of my life. It is the year my business has expanded, and expanded exponentially. We have doubled our work space over the past 3 years at our new location for Laser Spa

Group - expanding and taking over the lower level of the salon space. Our spa now has 4 private treatment rooms, a pedicure area, manicure station on the main level with prominent retail area, guest check-in and front desk, restroom, a staff room and full kitchen with laundry facilities. We have purchased several additional new lasers to add to the service menu - Fraxel, which is the gold standard in laser skin resurfacing. Whether you have sun damage, acne scarring, wrinkles, stretch marks, or want smoother skin, Fraxel delivers remarkable results and a fast recovery. We have also added a microdermabrasion machine, chemical peels, Botox, fillers, makeup applications, pedicures, manicures, waxing, eyelash extensions and many other services have also been added to the menu. I have also bought our second LightSheer Laser, as our original unit has a 2 month waiting list for treatments. We also added the BBL (BroadBand Light System) for Photo Rejuvenation, sun damage, broken vessels, fines lines and acne, the Silk Peel Dermalinfusion machine for luminous skin, and the Lumicell Wave 6 machine, for cellulite and body contouring. Laser tattoo removal will be coming soon.

We have our great neighbors Salon Michele offering hair salon services, in addition to our main level treatments offering full aesthetic treatments. We also now have 9 staff members and hired fabulous, friendly team players who give exceptional customer services which include 4 Medical Aestheticians a Receptionist, an R.N performing Cosmetic Filler Injections, an RMT (Registered Massage Therapist) for massages and a Micropigmentation Specialist to perform permanent makeup services, as well as a Makeup Artist and Eyelash Extensionist.

Seventeen years after I graduated from Aesthetics, I truly have a really great team working for me. I couldn't be happier.

Laser Spa Group has also been nominated for the Reader's Choice Awards for favourite laser hair removal business five years in a row. Laser Spa Group won the Platinum award in 2008 (first place), and Diamond in 2009 (second), and Platinum again in 2010. I have recently been Nominated Favourite Aesthetician and Favourite Medical Aesthetician 2010, 2011, Favourite Spa & Aesthetics as well as Favourite Laser Hair Removal 2011 and most recently I have won Favourite Aesthetician/Makeup Artist 2012.

Our laser rental program and laser training is in full swing and now rent several systems to qualified technicians.

I am currently looking to franchise my business and hope to find someone who will able to take me further along the right path. I want to implement our training with a template of growth and business plan for eager professionals entering the market.

We are in our early stages to plan our full institute of aesthetics, makeup artistry and medical aesthetics. We have all the technologies now under one roof and I'm ready to take my program, add additional curriculum and make it the best in the country.

I have been asked to be a clinical trainer for a laser company Xcite Technologies. Laser Spa Group refers customers to them for laser purchases and vice versa to me, for clinical training. We help buy, sell and rent LightSheer lasers to qualified buyers.

I just bought my very first brand new car, a Hyundai Santa Fe SUV, which is nice, safe and reliable for my son and I. On top of all of this, I also bought my first brand new home for myself and my son, and I am thrilled to finally settle in and rest my mind knowing that I will finally stay in one spot and call it home. I finally feel that I have found a place to stay and that the pieces of my life are coming together.

CHAPTER TWELVE

You can't connect the dots looking forward; you can only connect them looking backwards. So you have to trust that the dots will somehow connect in your future. You have to trust in something — your gut, destiny, life, karma, whatever. This approach has never let me down, and it has made all the difference in my life.
- Steve Jobs

Don't cry about money, It never cries for you.
- Kevin O'Leary

CONNECTING THE DOTS

If it had not been for my setbacks in my life, I wouldn't have been taken to my glorious moments. Despite what you may think, there is always a lesson to be learned and a future to make from any adversity.

Losing my father at a young age gives me greater compassion and comfort being a mother to my son. I don't let any precious moments go by. Dean gave me a son, Matteo, the most important aspect of my life and being a mother has been the most rewarding part of my life. I feel at peace amidst the prior chaos. My getting fired brought me to absorb myself into creating a course to teach laser and to better my business foundation, create my company from the ground up, and never forget what it was like to be the worker. It also made me realize I needed to be the leader and creator I had been all along. I have also made peace with Marc, we never spoke about what happened just ran into each other and discussed life as it was. Things feel better that way. Meeting Scorpio and Raphael sparked a fire that had always been inside me and showed me that with the right amount of courage and guidance I would be willing to do anything I believed in. That saga had also helped me finally end my abusive relationship with Amir. This new laser course I created brought me to my assistant, Silvana whom I feel a very special bond with and feel as though she is a sister to me. My lawsuits brought me courage to see things to the end, and I was strong enough through my prior experiences not to let it drag me down. I still kept moving on. My new location for my business has brought things full circle as I had known my friends there for over 20 years, and we have a great and solid foundation there. A new home, new car, new beginnings, surroundings and new wonders are waiting to be discovered.

I think too, if it wasn't for all these circumstances as well, that Sanjay my publisher wouldn't have noticed my journey to success. I wasn't born with a silver spoon in my mouth but it doesn't mean that I couldn't turn the clock forward, living for today, and improving my destiny, one baby step at a time.

Playing connect the dots as a child I could see myself staring at a new and complex page of dots and numbers in an art picture and trying to imagine what could possibly emerge from all that chaos. Today, as an adult I look forward in my life and try to imagine what future can possibly emerge from all the seeds that I may plant. Some things are easy to foresee. Some things are impossible to imagine and yet there is a marvel and mystery in what the future may hold.

In developing an appreciation for the lessons that life has already offered us, we will discover that happiness starts in the awareness that nothing which happens to or around us today is etched in stone. We are all empowered with the mind's option of *choice*. We can choose to dwell on today's challenges or blessings or we can begin to work towards a better tomorrow. Choice of happiness is a powerful option.

My story so far has been one of perseverance and fortitude. I have constantly battled to take control of life and to embrace its many opportunities. I've truly learned how to take things with grace, learn from each misgiving or misfortune, and to not get mad, just continue to stay grounded.

I think we should all strive for fortitude. I realize now that all these blurred moments of pain that seem so far away now, and all these inspirational new moments of my life, happening all at once, give me great joy and fulfillment. They are a part of the person that I am today. without the highs and the lows I would not be able to sit here now and write this book.

We all have to face adversity and we all need to find our saving grace, our little voice, our mother, father, brother, sister, confidante and keep listening. I know how to listen to the little voices now, and I don't have time for negativity or pretense. I use my instincts for most of my decisions. We do not have time to make all the mistakes that has helped to teach humanity its lessons, so I listen to the people that have gone through similar situations and take note.

I am finding new passions in my life and I hope one day to compete in a fitness competition as a new goal. I will be I will be forty soon and I feel the most fabulous I have ever felt. I would love to enter a half iron man race one day. Why not, the sky is the limit. Maybe that is crazy but there is a formula for success; there is a formula to get fit; and a formula to figure everything out in life. Listen to the experts, let it all sink in and deliver life the way it was supposed to be delivered. With passion and with love.

I feel young. I feel great. And I know so many women that can too. I've also decided to start modeling again and feel better today, than I ever did when I was so much younger. I love being creative and being in front of the camera. To take direction from a great photographer and create a beautiful image to evoke emotion captured in time for eternity is so rewarding. To be their muse and the spirit that is thought to inspire a poet or other artist; a source of genius or inspiration is priceless.

You can do anything that feels great, and at any age. If you wanted to start your business or build that dream don't let a number, or anyone hold you down. Surround yourself with like-minded people and embrace yourself in the wonders of your new vision. There are no formulas for living the life you secretly dream about, because if you simply accept and welcome life, it'll reveal itself to you. It is not through effort that you mould the universe to your liking, but from allowing the universe to mould you, and show you the way.

I used to be a big fan of working hard, really hard. I still work hard, but I do it from a place of inspiration and instinct, instead of necessity or just in motion. In the past few years, something has shifted within me, perhaps the birth of my son, finding my direction and settling down in both my home and business, and I cannot put my finger on exactly what is going on, but it seems to be happening in just the right way.

When I began doing what I love, which is showing my students how they themselves can be their own master, their own boss and to also help and service my clients, both men and women feel and look great about themselves, I never thought I had to take a predetermined path to my destination. I most love being behind the scenes in my business, and working all those long late night hours that no one else sees with planning, preparing and always visioning the bigger picture. No guidance counselor can show you what you love, you have to go through life and allow the universe to open up to you and catch all the opportunities that come your way, even though they may not be revealed as opportunities to you at first.

Circumstances may have almost stopped me, because I briefly didn't believe in myself or I second-guessed myself at different low points in my life. I saw so many others doing what I wanted to do, and they were more accomplished, had more knowledge, and were more successful. Or, so it seemed. I almost didn't stick things through to the end, but I'm glad I did.

I bought so many self-help books over the years and an entire library dedicated to self-awareness and fulfillment we are all in search of. Learning to let go, to really not only understand yourself, but others that are so close to you, and the many myriads that life has to offer. It is empowering to learn from others and find some kind of resonance with the words.

The early days were a struggle, but as I began seeing results, I started trusting myself more and more. I have in no way overcome any future obstacles, because life has its ups and downs. Problems come and go. Sometimes I'm more in tune with my inner wisdom, and sometimes I'm not, and on the days that I'm not, I do my best to relax and do something else. I always do my best creative work when I'm connected to that inner wisdom, and it is that inner wisdom that guides me towards the life I secretly dream about.

RELAX AND LEARN TO TRUST YOURSELF

I've always liked to plan myself into oblivion. I've felt the need to force progress, and force myself to keep moving forward whether I liked it or not. I have learned now to relax into the present moment. I notice what feelings and thoughts are present, and I relax into them, and try to stay connected with it.

There will be days where you feel like nothing is going wrong. Those are actually the most exciting days to stay in the present; because they help you grow your awareness of everything in the present moment. When I stay in the present, not only am I more connected to my inner solitude and wisdom, but I can feel relaxed that life is transpiring as it should so I do my best not to second guess. I don't like to blame anyone or anything for what is or isn't going on at the moment. It is what it is.

When you try and stay present, as best you can, you let life unfold in front of you. Sometimes it'll feel like chaos and the unknown inside of your body, but that's okay. It's the human experience we are all having and you may even want to try something new. Maybe your life is pushing you to experience something new. Connect with your inner wisdom and see how your life may travel in your new awareness.

Most people want logical answers and guarantees. They want to know that they'll get to realize their dreams. And I do, too, but those guarantees do not exist out there. Those guarantees exist within you. *You* are your own guarantee. When you learn to trust in yourself, you will quickly learn and naturally be led where you need to be. And sometimes it won't be pleasant, but as the Dalai Lama says: "Remember that sometimes not getting what you want is a wonderful stroke of luck."

You never know where that inner voice will lead you. It takes you on wonderful adventures, and you can make the adventure happen with courage, wisdom and your own self-reliance. The present moment will always be what you make of it. Be aware of how things transpired, and how they came to be. Because you are not your thoughts, you are the one who experiences it all. There is an inner wisdom within each and every one of us, and it is constantly guiding you to the life you secretly dream about living. It knows where to go. And it may guide you to a life that is even better than the one you secretly dream about.

If you want to live your dream life, learn to trust that inner voice. Learn to stay present, and learn to just be. There is no rush. There is only now.

A poem for Matteo

IF

If you can keep your head when all about you

Are losing theirs and blaming it on you,

If you can trust yourself when all men doubt you,

But make allowance for their doubting too;

If you can wait and not be tired by waiting,

Or being lied about, don't deal in lies,

Or being hated, don't give way to hating,

And yet don't look too good, nor talk too wise:

If you can dream - and not make dreams your master,

If you can think - and not make thoughts your aim;

If you can meet with Triumph and Disaster

And treat those two impostors just the same;

If you can bear to hear the truth you've spoken

Twisted by knaves to make a trap for fools,

Or watch the things you gave your life to, broken,

And stoop and build 'em up with worn-out tools:

If you can make one heap of all your winnings
And risk it all on one turn of pitch-and-toss,
And lose, and start again at your beginnings
And never breath a word about your loss;
If you can force your heart and nerve and sinew
To serve your turn long after they are gone,
And so hold on when there is nothing in you
Except the Will which says to them: "Hold on!"

If you can talk with crowds and keep your virtue,
Or walk with Kings - nor lose the common touch,
If neither foes nor loving friends can hurt you,
If all men count with you, but none too much;
If you can fill the unforgiving minute
With sixty seconds' worth of distance run,
Yours is the Earth and everything that's in it,
And - which is more - you'll be a Man, my son!

Rudyard Kipling (1865-1936)

PROFESSIONAL QUALIFICATIONS

As a trained and qualified aesthetician, I combine the art of healing with a sophisticated appreciation of aesthetics. I understand the subtle relationship between looking one's best and feeling one's best and am acutely aware of the power of perception and its significant contribution to the people's overall feeling of wellness.

I have developed my expertise by studying the field of Aesthetics and Cosmetology and receiving and Honours Diploma as an Aesthetician, Cosmetologist and Makeup Artist at the Alexandrian Institute. I received the distinguished honour of Student of the Year. The next field of study included Laser Hair Removal, in which I received Certification and training as a Certified Laser Specialist.

I am also certified as a Micropigmentation Specialist and Permanent Makeup Artist. I am certified in all Aveda Skin, Body, Lifestyle and Makeup Courses offered at Collega for Aveda, and have also been trained at the World's leading postgraduate facility, The International Dermal Institute for Dermalogica Skin Classes. I hold certification as Medical Aesthetician with Fraxel Lasers, Sciton BBLs (Broad Band Light) Technologies, SilkPeel Dermalinfusion, Vasculyse and Lumicell Wave 6 with Silhouete-Tone, Chemical Peels, Microdermabrasion, Laser Hair Removal with LightSheer with Clarion and certification in several M.A.C. Pro Master training classes including Editorial Makeup and Airbrushing Techniques. I was recognized as one of the Top 10 Makeup Artists in Canada by placing as a Finalist in *Canadian Hairdresser Magazine* for Makeup Artist of the Year 2001. I am certified as an Eyelash Extension Specialist. My latest field of study includes Spa Business, and I am a Certified Spa Director. I have also participated in several educational seminars and expositions including Aveda Congress in Minneapolis, webinars and educational seminars with Clarion and Lumenis.

My particular area of expertise is Laser Hair Removal and I opened my own company Laser Spa Group in 2003. I have developed a Laser Rental Program for Physicians, Clinics, Salons and Spas, and have created a research-friendly website detailing information in all aspects of laser hair removal, Brazilian waxing, hair growth cycles, hair growth disorders, and frequently asked questions. I have developed a 40 hour Laser & IPL Training course. Our training courses at Laser Spa Group are being designed to prepare the graduating student for the medical based aesthetic market. Courses are designed for those students with appropriate prerequisites, including aestheticians, nurses, cosmetologists, and physicians.

Laser Spa Group is Accredited with The BBB (Better Business Bureau), with the CFIB (Canadian Federation for Independent Business), and with the PGIB (Progressive Group for Independent Business).

I am an active member of the ASLMS (the American Society for Laser Medicine and Surgery) and the SCMHR (The Society for Clinical and Medical Hair Removal). My full biography has also been published and featured in the ABI - The American Biographical Institute's - Great Women of the 21st Century 2006 Edition.